Emerging Technologies

Foundation

Emerging Technologies

A Primer for Librarians

Jennifer Koerber
Michael P. Sauers

ROWMAN & LITTLEFIELD
Lanham • Boulder • New York • London

Published by Rowman & Littlefield
A wholly owned subsidary of The Rowman & Littlefield Publishing Group, Inc.
4501 Forbes Boulevard, Suite 200, Lanham, Maryland 20706
www.rowman.com

Unit A, Whitacre Mews, 26-34 Stannary Street, London SE11 4AB

British Library Cataloguing in Publication Information Available

Library of Congress Cataloging-in-Publication Data

Koerber, Jennifer.
   Emerging technologies : a primer for librarians / Jennifer Koerber, Michael P. Sauers.
      pages cm
   Includes bibliographical references and index.
   ISBN 978-1-4422-3887-9 (hardcover : alk. paper) — ISBN 978-1-4422-3888-6 (pbk. :
alk. paper) — ISBN 978-1-4422-3889-3 (ebook)
   1. Libraries—Information technology. I. Sauers, Michael P., 1970–. II. Title.
Z678.9.S33 2015
025.00285—dc23   2015002398

∞™ The paper used in this publication meets the minimum requirements of
American National Standard for Information Sciences—Permanence of Paper
for Printed Library Materials, ANSI/NISO Z39.48-1992.

Printed in the United States of America

Contents

Acknowledgments

My first thanks must go to my coauthor, Michael—a short conversation about a power strip led to years of friendship and our first collaboration on this work. Thanks for getting me into and out of this one, sir.

I'd also like to thank Charles Harmon, our editor at Rowman & Littlefield, for his confidence in the success of this book and all of his guidance getting here.

To Meghan Weeks (Boston Public Library, MA), Henry Bankhead (Los Gatos Public Library, CA), Matthew Clark (Provincetown Public Library, MA), Kelvin Watson (Queens Public Library, NY), Lauren Comito (Queens Public Library, NY), Rivkah Sass (Sacramento Public Library, CA), Gerald Ward (Sacramento Public Library, CA), Jim Azevedo (Smashwords), and Dolores Greenwald (Williamson County Public Library, TN)—my thanks for your excellent work and your patient responses to my requests.

My dear friends and family, thank you for supporting me in all I've done, including this current madness; most especially Jessica Steytler, best friend and provider of calming words and bright levity.

And to Matt Ringel—husband, photographer, first and last reader of every word, and one-man cheering squad. Thank you, always.

—Jennifer Koerber

Thanks to Charles for his continuing faith in my ability to get things done (mostly) on time; my coauthor, Jennifer, for joining me for this one; and to David Lee King (Topeka and Shawnee County Public Library, KS), Jake Rundle (Hastings Public Library, NE), Martina Soden (Scranton Public Library, PA), Ronelle Miller-Hood (Cleveland Public Library, OH), and Tiffany Harkleroad (Ford City Public Library, PA) for their contributions to the project.

—Michael P. Sauers

Introduction

Welcome to *Emerging Technologies*.

First, let's deal with an obvious question: Why a print book on emerging technologies? We wanted to take a snapshot of the new technologies that are becoming increasingly important to libraries and use these examples to illustrate how to look at the technology of the next decade, next year, or even next week.

In each chapter, we offer a brief overview of background information and current events followed by a list of advantages and challenges to using technologies in a library setting. We highlight the most useful or most well-known tools and devices, then specify how libraries might use these technologies. Finally, we look at a variety of current examples from libraries in the United States and around the globe.

By breaking down six different kinds of technology in this way, we're giving you a model to use to look at any new technology, consider its relevance to your field of librarianship, and brainstorm how you might use it now or in the near future.

This print book will be complemented and supplemented by an enhanced e-book version featuring video interviews with some of the librarians mentioned here, as well as with additional experts in the various fields we cover. These interviews are also available at http://www.travelinlibrarian.info/EmergingTechnologies.

What do we mean by *emerging*? The technologies we cover in this book are just hitting the middle of the acceptance bell curve. Nothing so cutting edge that only a few people even understand it and nothing so mainstream that everyone is using it. We also look at older technology being used in new ways, using very recent advances to change what's possible using that tool.

What do we mean by *technology*? For the most part, we mean physical technology: gadgets, hardware, devices, controllers, gizmos; whatever you like to call the physical thing you hold in your hand. However, we do include a few "back-end" technological advances that completely change how people interact with library services, in particular the global connections and economies of scale made possible by the Internet for self-publishing (chapter 2) and fund-raising (chapter 4).

Why did we choose these particular topics? We limited our scope to technologies we either knew were being used in libraries already or had a good chance of affecting library services and programming in the very near future. In addition, we wanted to focus on topics that one or both of us could speak on with familiarity, all the way down to using these technologies ourselves or in our own libraries.

BOOK ORGANIZATION

The first four chapters—"Audio and Video," "Self-Publishing and the Library as Publisher," "Mobile Technologies," and "Crowdfunding"—all look at older technologies that are reinvented and reimagined through significant advances in quality, scale, or hardware. Many libraries were already using these technologies in some way and are now able to change and adapt those uses to meet current needs and take advantage of the latest improvements.

In chapter 1, we start things off with technologies that are emerging in the library world: audio and video. Although both of these technologies have been around for a very long time, today's near ubiquity of computers and the Internet is prompting libraries to find new uses for audio and video, from event promotion to content delivery.

Chapter 2 also looks at older technologies, from online retail to the humble photocopier, and shows how the popularity of e-books and the ability to move large files quickly across the Internet has revolutionized small presses and self-publishing. Most importantly, we'll see that the public library is finally poised to become a true center for community authorship.

Chapter 3 reviews the basics of mobile technologies and shows how advances in both hardware and software are making it easier for libraries to serve users at any level of technology knowledge and availability.

In chapter 4, we switch gears and take a look at crowdfunding, a method for gathering the funds necessary to achieve that special project that doesn't fit into your existing budget.

With chapter 5, we turn our attention to technologies that are pushing the envelope when it comes to the cutting edge: wearables. From fitness bands to virtual reality headsets, wearables have a lot of potential to change the way libraries both gather and disseminate data.

Chapter 6 continues the journey to the future via the Internet of Things: simple but powerful computers that can be embedded into everyday objects and connected to controllers or data aggregation tools. It seems like science fiction, but it's already here.

The last two chapters—"Privacy and Security" and "Keeping Up with Emerging Technology"—are all-purpose topics that will continue to be affected by new developments in technology. In chapter 7, we begin to wind down by taking a look at the latest issues and technologies involved in privacy and security, since every technology presented in the first six chapters has implications in both of these areas. Chapter 8 offers a wide variety of ways to stay on top of innovations in technology and computing. Keeping up is vital to libraries, both to serve the existing needs of library users and to anticipate what's coming next.

As you read this book, it might be helpful to keep a few questions in mind:

- Since early 2015, what has changed about the technologies discussed in this book? How have libraries found new ways to incorporate those changes into their services?
- Have any of these gadgets or platforms become mainstream enough (again) to fade into the background of "everyone's doing it?" What is commonplace when you're reading this that was emerging when we wrote the book?
- In the past year or so, what completely unexpected innovation came out of left field and changed everything?
- Are patrons using the technology in ways that the library will need to adapt to? How quickly will libraries need to get up to speed to catch up to their users?
- How do you think libraries might use the technology directly? Through programs and services or just by being aware enough to answer questions?

We hope that through the examples we've presented, as well as others you'll find in the e-book version and future updates, you'll get a better sense of how to keep track of what's next in technology for libraries and how to handle it when it comes.

Chapter One

Audio and Video

HOW ARE AUDIO AND VIDEO "EMERGING" TECHNOLOGIES?

Chances are that you're asking yourself this question right now. It's not like audio and video technologies are something new. However, we've found that with the amount of inexpensive audio and video recording technology available today—you might have a miniature recording studio in your pocket right now—both audio and video are "emerging" in the sense that many libraries are just starting to take advantage of these technologies. With this increasing availability and decreasing cost, we decided that it would be a great place to start. You'll see this again in the self-publishing and mobile chapters: new ways of imagining or using existing older technologies.

You could easily write a whole book on how audio and video can be used and exactly how to do it in a library setting. However, since we have just this one chapter, we'll be giving you an overview of the equipment and software involved, providing plenty of examples as to how to use them in your library.

PROS AND CONS

We are firm believers in the use of audio and video both to distribute information and to publicize the library. As we've already mentioned, the availability of tools and platforms at little to no cost, along with the overall near ubiquity of the medium these days, makes this a technology that libraries would be remiss in ignoring. Just look at the number of videos uploaded to YouTube—"100 hours of video are uploaded to YouTube every minute" and "over 6 billion hours of video are watched each month on YouTube."[1] It's an incredibly popular medium.

The only downside we see is that of time. From planning to recording to editing, creating reasonably well-done and entertaining media that people will watch will take time. Though some of the software tools are easier to learn than others, they all have a learning curve. But as with most things, with time the process will get easier and faster. There are many things you can do to reduce that time, the most important of which is to repurpose content you already have. Does your library host public events like speakers and book readings? If so, record them. Once you have the recording, the editing of those events will generally be minimal (e.g., adding titles and credits), and once that's done, you can not only easily publish the video online but also quickly turn the audio of the recording into a podcast or stand-alone downloadable audio programming.

When it comes to audio and video production, you're going to need hardware, software, and a platform to put it on—one item from each category. Within each category there are several choices and which you choose is, in many cases, less a budgetary concern (though ultimately your budget will need to be considered) and more based on what it is you're trying to accomplish. For example, if you're looking to do a screencast (i.e., record what's on a computer screen in order to create a tutorial for someone to watch later), a $3,000 professional camera will be useless, or at the very least overkill, and a $50 webcam would be a better choice, assuming you want your smiling face to be seen as part of the recording. In the next two sections, we'll talk more about the types of equipment needed for different types of projects.

HARDWARE

A Computer

At some point in the process you're going to need a computer, whether to do the actual recording (see the previously mentioned screencasting example) or when you get to the editing process. These days, any current desktop or laptop computer will have the underlying hardware necessary to edit and process high-definition (HD) video. But there are some things you should consider: First, if you're only working with audio, you won't need nearly as much power. Second, if you plan on doing a lot of work with video, a dedicated computer with a large monitor, lots of RAM (random-access memory), and a multicore CPU (central processing unit) will make your life a lot easier.

Cameras

In order to record video, you'll need a video camera. There are five basic types to choose from:

Your Phone

If you have a smartphone made in the past few years, chances are it will do a relatively good job of recording high-definition video. The downside to this sort of camera is generally a lack of stability—that is, they're not easily attached to tripods without additional adapters.

Webcams

An HD webcam such as the Microsoft LifeCam (figure 1.1) will cost somewhere between $30 and $75 depending on the resolution you need. These are perfect for "talking head" screencasting, recording online events like a Google hangout, or recording directly into YouTube. Your laptop may also have a built-in webcam, but be sure to check its supported resolution, as many are not HD.

Figure 1.1. Microsoft LifeCam.

Digital Cameras

Most digital cameras sold today, whether a point-and-shoot or DSLR (digital single-lens reflective camera), include the ability to record HD video ranging in cost from $150 to more than $1,000 for a professional-level DSLR with interchangeable lenses. These are a great alternative for someone who wants more stability than a smartphone camera but also wants the flexibility to be able to use it as a still camera.

Digital Video Cameras

These days a dedicated video camera can cost anywhere from $100 to $2,000 depending on the features you're looking for. A small Sony handheld camera that can record HD video to a microSD card generally runs about $190, while a JVC professional HD camera that records to a MiniDV tape and has an external boom microphone will cost about $1,500 (figure 1.2). Those with significant cash to spare can even go for an UltraHD (4k) camera, starting around $5,000. The benefits of the higher-end cameras include better microphones, more control over functions such as focus and zoom, and the ability to use the camera as a webcam with the right connecting cables.

Figure 1.2.   The Nebraska Library Commission's Canon XH-A1S video camera.

Microphones

If you're looking to record audio programming, you have a few options when it comes to microphones and their connections to your other equipment. Let's take a look, starting with the lowest quality and working our way up.

Built-in. Most tablets or laptops come with a built-in microphone. While these will work for things like Skype calls and will have reasonable sound quality, we highly recommend that you don't use these for recording purposes. It may sound fine to you now, but as you start working with better microphones, you'll quickly hear the difference.

3.5 mm jack. These are external microphones that connect to your computer using the same size jack that your headphones use (figure 1.3). While these microphones will be better than the one built into your laptop, we still recommend avoiding these as they rely on the sound quality of your computer's built-in audio processing and, if you're using whatever came with your computer's motherboard, chances are the quality will be poor.

USB. Here we're starting to work with some great microphones while not spending a lot of money. In most cases, USB-connected microphones that

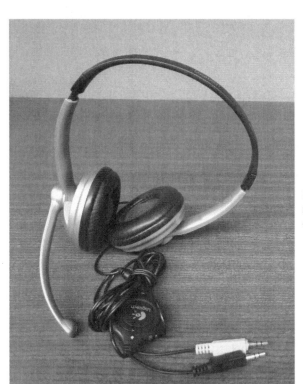

Figure 1.3. Headset microphone with 3.5 mm connector.

Figure 1.4. Blue Snowball (left) and Blue Yeti (right) microphones.

have audio processing built in are of much better quality than the microphone built into your computer. With USB microphones, you have the option between headset microphones—which are great if you're not also on camera—or standalone microphones such as the Blue Snowball or Yeti (figure 1.4), which will give you great sound quality for around $100.

XLR. XLR-connected microphones are professional grade and are large, round locking connectors with three pins (figure 1.5). These are the type of microphones that you see being used in a recording studio or on a stage. These microphones don't have to be prohibitively expensive, but computers do not come with these types of connections, so you'll need to purchase additional equipment, such as a mixing board, which will increase your costs.

SOFTWARE

When it comes to software, what you'll need again depends on the type of recording you're doing. You have many options, so we'll just focus on a few options in each scenario.

Figure 1.5. Microphone with XLR connector. David Lee King, used with permission.

Screencasting and Live Events

Online Services

There are a few different online services that allow you to record your screen. The one that we've had the most success with is Screencast-O-Matic (http://www.screencast-o-matic.com/; figure 1.6). There are both free and paid versions available. The free version limits you to fifteen minutes of recording time and places a watermark on your recordings, but it does get the job done and is a great solution if you're not willing or able to install software on the computer you're using. (Screencast-O-Matic also has a downloadable/installable version with similar limitations.)

Local Software

If you're looking for some powerful screencasting software, both TechSmith Camtasia (http://www.techsmith.com/camtasia.html) and Adobe Captivate (http://www.adobe.com/products/captivate.html) are popular options. Both of these packages have current list prices of $299 and $29.99 per month,

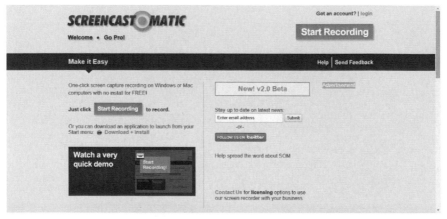

Figure 1.6.   Screencast-O-Matic.

respectively. Generally, we recommend these if you're looking for something to support full-fledged online learning environments.

Live Event Platforms

If you want to create recordings of online events, three of your options are GoToWebinar (http://www.gotomeeting.com/online/webinar), Google Hangouts (https://plus.google.com/hangouts), and TalkShoe (http://www.talkshoe .com/talkshoe/). GoToWebinar is great for online presentations where the presenter shares a screen with the attendees. The recordings of the events are then made available in a .WMV format. Pricing currently starts at $79 per month for one hundred attendees, and the platform has a free thirty-day trial.

Google Hangouts is a better solution if you have multiple presenters who wish to speak to the camera. The system can handle switching from presenter to presenter depending on who's talking. Recordings are automatically saved to an associated YouTube account, and the service is free.

TalkShoe (figure 1.7) is a free online podcast service for audio recording. Participants call into a TalkShoe phone number or connect via voice-over IP (VoIP), and the conversation is recorded. Audio files can be downloaded from the service and hosted on your own server, or you can use TalkShoe's built-in hosting.

Video Editing

Once you have your recording, you'll probably need to do some basic editing to your file, such as adding titles and credits. If you're doing something such as a book talk where the speaker has had to do multiple takes to fix speaking

Figure 1.7. TalkShoe.

errors or a more complex video with multiple shots, you'll be working in your video-editing software more extensively. While whole books have been written on the concepts of video editing, we will give you an overview of some of the more common options.

Windows Movie Maker (http://windows.microsoft.com/en-us/ windows-live/movie-maker)

This is the default, free video-editing program for Windows (figure 1.8). Depending on which version of Windows you're running, you may already have

Figure 1.8. Windows Movie Maker.

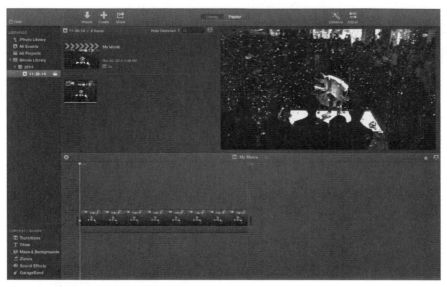

Figure 1.9.   iMovie.

it. (It may also be titled "Windows Live Movie Maker" in some Windows versions.) While it doesn't have every possible feature available in more complex programs, it has enough to get most jobs done.

iMovie (https://www.apple.com/mac/imovie/)

This is the Apple equivalent of Windows Movie Maker and comes with current versions of Mac OS (figure 1.9). As with Movie Maker, it doesn't have a lot of fancy features but is enough for most common, less involved projects.

Final Cut Pro (http://www.apple.com/final-cut-pro/)

You can think of this program as the professional version of iMovie. With a list price of $299, this is video-editing software for someone who wants to do pretty much anything and everything with video on a Mac (figure 1.10).

Lightworks (http://www.lwks.com/)

Lightworks is a free, full-feature video-editing package available for Windows, Mac, and Linux platforms (figure 1.11). This is a great option for someone looking for a complete video-editing package that will work across platforms and will have no budget impact. A paid pro version is also available under a subscription and purchase model, with a current list price of $174.99 for a year's license.

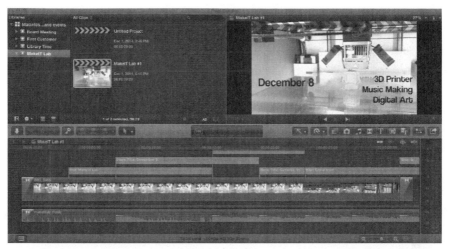

Figure 1.10. Final Cut Pro.

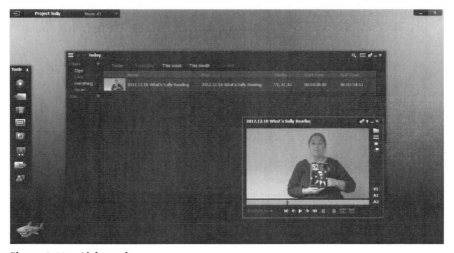

Figure 1.11. Lightworks.

Audio Editing

If you're working with audio-only projects or are looking to tweak the audio for your video files, you also have a number of options. However, there are two that are currently the most popular. GarageBand (https://www.apple .com/mac/garageband/) is your default option if you're a Mac user since it comes with Mac OS. Audacity (http://audacity.sourceforge.net/) is an open-source, cross-platform program (figure 1.12). We've used both of these programs, and from a functionality standpoint, they're pretty much the same.

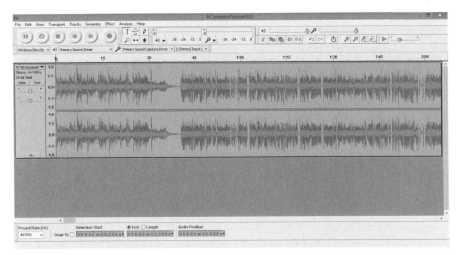

Figure 1.12. Audacity.

PLATFORMS

Once you have your completed audio or video file, you'll need a place to host it. In many cases, you may wish to self-host your content on the library's web server. Although this often seems like a great default option, it may not be the best choice. For example, unless your web server also has the necessary software to stream audio/video content, users may need to download a very large video file before being able to play it. On the other hand, if you use YouTube to host your content, features like streaming, automatic quality adjustment, embedding, and commenting are supplied by default. Before deciding where to host your files, be sure to decide what you'd like your patrons to do with those files.

Here are a few of your options:

YouTube (https://www.youtube.com/)

YouTube is the default platform for video sharing. With its ability to accept nearly any video format as an upload and convert it into an easily streamable format in multiple resolutions, it is very difficult to choose a different plat-form. Add to that the built-in commenting and sharing features, and YouTube is the choice of almost every library we've spoken to.

Vimeo (https://vimeo.com/)

Vimeo is very similar to YouTube but prides itself on being a platform for more serious, high-quality, ad-free video content. Vimeo has multiple levels of accounts, ranging from a free basic account to Vimeo Pro. Each subsequent level offers more bandwidth, better support, and increased analytics.

Ustream (http://www.ustream.tv/)

Ustream is a platform for both creating and storing your video content. Each account gives you the ability to directly stream live content through the service via webcam with a built-in chat functionality for viewers. Post-event, Ustream offers the ability to download and/or archive your content for later viewing. Both of us have attended and viewed conference sessions that have been streamed via Ustream. The service offers a free, ad-supported version along with several levels of paid accounts, which include increased bandwidth, storage, and quality.

SoundCloud (https://soundcloud.com/)

If you want to store and deliver your audio content on a free cloud service, SoundCloud is currently the most popular. You can think of it as a YouTube for audio content. Once you've created your content, upload it to your SoundCloud account and give users the ability to subscribe to, embed, download, and/or comment on your content.

There's one last thing we'd like to mention in this section: what to do with all of that old analog content in order to make it available digitally. In this case, your solution is an "analog capture device" such as Honestech's VHS to DVD Deluxe (http://www.honestech.com/) at a list price of $79 (figure 1.13). This is a small box that allows you to connect an analog audio or video

Figure 1.13. Honestech's VHS to DVD Deluxe.

source, such as a turntable or VHS player, as input and then output via USB cable to software on your computer. You then play the source material and record it digitally. Typically, the box will come with its own recording software, but it is also compatible with other programs such as Audacity.

USES

As we discussed each of your hardware, software, and platform options, we mentioned a few different scenarios in which you might use them. Now let's take a step back from the equipment specifics and take a look at the many different ways that you might be able to use these options to provide services to your patrons. These are just ideas to get you thinking about the possibilities. In the next section, we will provide you with several specific examples.

Introducing the Library

Patrons that are new to town or campus may be interested in knowing what's available at the library. How about a video tour? This would be especially helpful for older university libraries with architectural features such as half-floors. Why not expand outside of the library to the campus or town and offer a downloadable audio walking tour that people can listen to on their phones?

Training

Screencasts are perfect for training someone on how to use a computer, even if it is just to perform a simple task. It's one thing to provide a step-by-step instruction sheet, but how about providing a video walkthrough first? This way trainees can become familiar with the process before attempting it themselves.

Memes

Have you ever heard the term *viral video*? Many viral videos are those that are participating in a larger meme, an idea that passes itself around like a virus. From Pharrell Williams's "Happy" to PSY's "Gangnam Style," from the Harlem Shake to the Rickroll, libraries can participate in a video meme just as easily as anyone else. The fun part is that we get to both participate in the latest craze and promote the library at the same time.

Community Engagement

This one is pretty broad and has a lot of possibilities. One of the best ways you can use audio and video to directly engage your community is through a community oral history project. If the library has the equipment, invite community members into the library to record their memories; a local Story-Corps.[2] If your equipment is mobile (e.g., a laptop and a microphone), take it out into the community instead of insisting that the people come to you.

Events

This is the one that we would consider a no-brainer as most of the work has already been done. If you're holding an event at your library, record it and make it available for later viewing by those who wish to relive the experience or who missed it. Some events will work great in an audio-only format while others will easily lend themselves to video. The one thing to keep in mind is that you will need to get permission from the person actually doing the event. While some speakers will happily allow you to post a recording, others will not. (If you do record, you'll want to notify attendees that you are doing so and that by attending the event they acknowledge that they may be included in the finished product.)

Supporting Makers

When it comes to supporting makers, this is the application that is the most "emerging" when it comes to libraries and will most likely take the largest outlay of money to accomplish. In this case, instead of the library being the sole user of the equipment, the library makes the equipment available in a studio space for use by the library's patrons. Some libraries are starting to offer separate bookable audio and video recording studios with professional-level equipment and software and in some cases even a "green screen" wall that users can take advantage of.

LIBRARY EXAMPLES

NCompass Live and the *NCompass Podcast* (http://nlc.nebraska.gov/NCompassLive/ and https://itunes.apple.com/us/podcast/ncompass-audio-video-covering/id576497533)

NCompass Live is the Nebraska Library Commission's weekly online event, covering a variety of library activities and topics. The show is free and open to anyone to watch. These one-hour sessions are hosted by Christa Burns, the NLC's Special Projects Librarian, every Wednesday at 10:00AM (CT) and include a mixture of presentations, interviews, book reviews, Web tours, mini training sessions, and Q and A sessions presented by NLC staff and guest speakers. Attendees ask questions and participate in the show via VoIP, using their own microphone, or in the live text chat.[3]

The *NCompass Podcast* is a (mostly) audio podcast made up of content from both the *NCompass Live* show and recordings of other events put on by the Nebraska Library Commission. Live episodes are recorded using GoToWebinar, a Blue Snowball microphone, and a Canon XH-A1S camera. Videos are uploaded to YouTube and the Internet Archive. Audio-only versions are created using VLC (for converting video files to audio files), Levelator (for leveling the audio of multiple participants), and Audacity.

T Is for Training (http://tisfortraining.wordpress.com/)

T is for Training is an informal podcast dedicated to but not obsessed with training in libraries. Started in 2008 by baldgeekinmd [Maurice Coleman], this program seeks to deepen the conversation about training, share resources, connect, socially network, and to laugh a lot. So, grab a beverage of your choice and join us either live or via podcast. Episodes are recorded live using TalkShoe.[4]

Voter Voices (http://votervoices.blogspot.com/)

"Campaign Connection 2012: Voter Voices" is a unique NET News election-year project. At libraries and other locations throughout the state, we're gathering your thoughts, perspective and questions to share with the candidates, and the rest of Nebraska, on television, radio, web and social media.[5]

NET Nebraska staff worked with Nebraska Library Commission staff to set up a process where citizens could sit down at computers in public libraries and other locations around the state and record a video question directly into YouTube via a webcam. Throughout the length of the project, more than thirty videos were created and some were featured on a "Voter Voices Television Special" where US Senate candidates responded to some of the questions that had been submitted.

Nebraska Libraries on the Web Training (http://libraries.ne.gov/)

One of the projects that Michael runs at the Nebraska Library Commission is Nebraska Libraries on the Web (http://libraries.ne.gov/), a WordPress-based hosting solution for more than seventy public library websites across the state. After an initial round of live training, all of the training is currently done via screencasts of Michael performing many of the most common tasks involved in using WordPress. All of the videos are created using Microsoft

Expression Encoder 4 and uploaded to YouTube. The videos are then embedded on the Online Training page of the project's website for anyone to view and comment on.

AV Studio at the Topeka and Shawnee County Public Library, Topeka, KS, by David Lee King, Digital Services Director, Topeka and Shawnee County Public Library

The Topeka and Shawnee County Public Library opened the MakeIT Lab on December 8, 2014. The library's goal is to help customers create through three services: a digital media studio, four "media bags" that can be checked out, and a 3-D printer. This technology will allow customers to create a variety of content, including creating, editing, and sharing videos; scanning, touching up, and sharing photos; creating a brochure or flyer for a small business; recording music, podcasts, and oral histories; converting old home videos into digital formats; and sharing their creations with the library, tagged "made at the library."

Equipment includes two Apple iMac computers, Apple's iLife Software (GarageBand and iMovie), microphones, a USB twenty-five-key keyboard, studio monitors, digital cameras and camcorders, an analog-to-digital audio converter, a video converter, and a MakerBot Replicator 3-D printer.

The library plans to measure success of the pilot project by tracking media room use, media bag checkouts, and program attendance.

Volume Denver, Denver Public Library (https://volumedenver .org), by Zeth Lietzau, Manager, Digital User Experience and Community Technology Center, Denver Public Library

Volume is a local music website from the Denver Public Library (DPL) that seeks to connect the members of the community with the vibrant music scene there. It features Colorado-based musicians who, in addition to the small license fee that the library can offer, receive exposure to an audience they might not otherwise reach. DPL cardholders can log in to the site to download full tracks and albums, DRM-free. Cardholders can also stream full tracks and create playlists of their favorite local bands. People without DPL cards are limited to thirty-second streaming samples of the tracks.

Volume is built atop the Drupal content management system and uses jPlayer, a jQuery plug-in, to stream the music using HTML5 audio. In addition to these open-source options, DPL staff wrote custom Drupal modules and theme functionality, primarily in PHP and JavaScript, to achieve the desired functionality.

John F. Englert Collection's Oral Histories, Ford City Public Library, Ford City, PA (http://www.armstronglibraries.org/ ford-city/history/), by Tiffany Harkleroad, Program Coordinator, Ford City Public Library

The Ford City Public Library is a small, rural library located in Ford City, Pennsylvania. The community was once the company town for Pittsburgh Plate Glass, now PPG Industries, and because of this, there was a rich heritage that we wanted to preserve as a part of the library collection. The library began collecting oral histories of community members, focusing on those who had lived through the Great Depression and World War II, and continues to work on growing the collection to capture oral histories from different decades. The oral histories are collected on video via a Canon VIXIA HF R300, as well as in audio form via a Marantz Professional Solid State Recorder. Raw video files are converted and imported into Windows Movie Maker, where they are edited. Video files are then saved on external hard drive and burned to a DVD. The audio is transcribed with an Olympus AS-2400 Transcription Kit, and copies of audio files are burned onto a CD. DVDs, CDs, and transcripts are then added to the library's circulating collection. Patrons can check these out or use them in the library. Additionally, edited video files are uploaded to the library's YouTube channel, where the public at large can view them. Finally, all files are added to an entry page and linked to the oral history collection on the Ford City Public Library's webpage.

Natural Disasters in NePA: Hurricane Diane, the Lackawanna Valley Digital Archives Team (http://www. lackawannadigitalarchives.org/), by Martina Soden, MLIS, Head of Reference Services, Scranton Public Library, Scranton, PA

This is a digital collection of eighty-five photographs, monographs, audio and video interviews, and TV footage focusing on Hurricane Diane which, in August 1955, devastated sections of the city of Scranton. Video interviews with witnesses were recorded on a Panasonic SDR-H40P camcorder with a small, table-top tripod in the Scranton Public Library's Community Room. The onboard microphone was used for recording and the recordings were saved to the camcorder as a MOD file and then transcoded to MPEG4 using MPEG Streamclip. The MPEG4 was uploaded to YouTube and is streamed from there. One witness was not local and was therefore interviewed by phone via a telephone conferencing system and the interview was recorded using a digital audio recorded to a WAV file. An MP3 copy was also produced using Audacity. The file is streamed from the library's web server. WGBI-TV footage was digitized from 16mm open reel by SceneSavers to uncompressed

AVI. A compressed MPEG4 was also created and is streamed from YouTube. Copies of all master files and surrogates are stored on the library's server and backed up on a regular basis.

Craft Shop (https://www.youtube.com/watch?v=BV7OagqPqns &feature=youtu.be), by Royce Kitts, Library Director, Liberal Memorial Library, Liberal, KS

My experience with making videos for libraries is one filled with fun, failure, and success. The videos I have made in the past fall into two main categories: informative and goofiness. When working with video, there are a couple of rules that I try to live by: (1) Make sure to have fun making the video. (2) Don't try to make it perfect.

The key to creating an effective video is to keep the message simple and keep the video short. I use videos as a way to make patrons laugh but at the same time educate them on the services we have at the library. Videos are a great way to preserve and distribute an archive of an event that has happened at the library.

My favorite video was one I made to highlight the craft equipment and supplies that were available at the library. At the time the song "Thrift Shop" by Macklemore was really popular and my son just made a parody version based on MineCraft. In a moment of inspiration, I thought to do a video about our craft area and titled the project "Craft Shop." I found a free instrumental version of the song and wrote a rap to go with the video. A couple of staff members and I scripted the video out on a piece of copy paper and within twenty minutes were shooting a video using our Flip cams.[6] I am a big fan of iMovie and, for some smaller projects, Windows Movie Maker. Both have their merits depending on the project, and both are cheap and/or free. Both have a small learning curve and are less intimidating than more professional products. After about an hour of editing, the video was up on YouTube and embedded on the library's homepage.

Project-based work in libraries can scare people. We all know how some can go on forever. My advice is to keep the process simple so that you are willing to make another video without fear. Making a good video is a lot more fun than making a perfect video.

NOTES

1. "Statistics," YouTube, accessed August 22, 2014, https://www.youtube.com/yt/press/statistics.html.

2. "Since 2003, StoryCorps has collected and archived more than 50,000 interviews with over 90,000 participants. Each conversation is recorded on a CD to share,

and is preserved at the American Folklife Center at the Library of Congress. Story-Corps is one of the largest oral history projects of its kind, and millions listen to our weekly broadcasts on NPR's *Morning Edition* and on our Listen pages." "About Us," StoryCorps, accessed February 25, 2015, http://storycorps.org/about.

3. *"NCompass Live,"* Nebraska Library Commission, accessed February 25, 2015, http://nlc.nebraska.gov/NCompassLive/.

4. *"T Is for Training,"* TalkShoe, accessed February 25, 2015, http://www.talk shoe.com/talkshoe/web/talkCast.jsp?masterId=24719&cmd=tc.

5. "Campaign Connection 2012: Voter Voices," NET Nebraska, accessed February 25, 2015, http://www.netnebraska.org/basic-page/news/campaign-connection-2012.

6. The Flip Video series of cameras was discontinued in 2012. "Flip Video," *Wikipedia*, accessed February 25, 2015, http://en.wikipedia.org/wiki/Flip_Video.

Chapter Two

Self-Publishing and the Library as Publisher

WHAT'S NEW IN SELF-PUBLISHING?

Self-publishing has been around longer than the modern publishing industry. Before Gutenberg's press revolutionized printing, if you wrote (by hand) and sold a second copy of something you'd written, you were technically self-publishing. In the modern era, small publishers, vanity presses, and desktop publishing software made creating and distributing a book progressively easier.

In the twenty-first century, authors now have the ability to publish and distribute their work on a global scale and readers are able to find these books easily (figure 2.1). Authors can create e-books and make them available on their own websites, or they can use self-publishing platforms like Smash-words, Lulu, or Amazon's suite of services to sell their works around the world. Readers can use those same platforms to find popular titles or small niche works on their own interests.

The basics of self-publishing are straightforward: Authors write their books in a word-processing program, then they edit, format, and design the book (including the cover) themselves or hire other people to do it for them. If the author is also the illustrator or photographer, he or she can add images directly to the document or use a paid service to make sure the final product looks professional.

Once the book is ready, authors have two primary choices to distribute or sell it. They can use software or online tools to convert their document into a print- or e-book-ready format (ePUB, MOBI/AZW, AZW3/KF8, iBooks, PDF, or others) and make the files available directly on their own website, or they can upload their book to an online distributor to give it the broadest possible exposure and offer print copies through a print-on-demand (POD) service. After the book is published, the author is responsible for generating

Figure 2.1. Self-published titles come in all formats, both print and digital.

word-of-mouth marketing through social media, interviews, book trailers, and any other means they can find to sell copies.

The obvious difference between self-publishing and traditional publishing is that the author is entirely responsible for all the work that goes into making the book. However, some of the biggest online distributors are also full-service self-publishing platforms, offering editorial, design, and even basic marketing assistance to a solo author.

As we'll see in the library examples, libraries are getting involved in self-publishing at every stage from purchasing self-published books to supporting authors with programs and workshops to starting publishing imprints run by the library itself.

PROS AND CONS

For both authors and readers, there are pros and cons to self-publishing, but the increasing numbers of successful self-published authors indicate that the drawbacks are disappearing.

Self-publishing allows many more authors to have the opportunity to see their works in print, increasing the diversity of voices and subjects available to readers. Small niche markets focusing on highly specialized topics can thrive, and local histories and personal stories from a broader range of views can be shared. Without having to support the business of a traditional publisher, authors can keep a higher percentage of the profits, so even if they sell fewer copies overall, they make more money on each copy.

On the other hand, without the oversight and curation of traditional publishers, readers have to work harder to find high-quality, engaging books. Even well-written works might be unreadable due to subpar, distracting layouts and designs. Also, self-publishing creates a tremendous amount of work for an author, taking up time that might otherwise be spent working on the next book.

As self-publishing platforms expand their services and as better tools are available to authors, it's easier and more affordable for authors either to do the nonwriting work of creating their books or to pay others to fill in the gaps in their skills. This is improving the overall quality of self-published books and improving the genre.

For libraries, there are pros and cons both to buying self-published works and providing services to support self-publishing authors. Buying self-published books means more diverse and locally relevant content in library collections and the opportunity for local authors to use their local library as a launch pad for their books. However, until there are more centralized clearinghouses or distribution networks for self-published authors, collection development staff could be overloaded trying to find high-quality self-published works.

A primary benefit to offering library programs and services to support self-publishing is increasing engagement with local communities of writers, editors, designers, photographers, and other creators. In addition, these same programs can serve multiple populations—local history authors, genealogists, niche scholars, students, incarcerated or homebound populations, and so on. The dangers lie in overcommitting library staff to support these programs and underdelivering on the services you promise to provide. It's also risky to make a large purchase, such as an Espresso Book Machine or other POD technology, and then not have sufficient use in order to justify the expense.

Nonacademic libraries are also beginning to take the extra step and become publishers in their own right. For these libraries, the risks range from staff overload to copyright infringement by and of authors, while the benefits include the opportunity to throw the weight of the library's name behind the work of local creators and to encourage libraries and communities to invest in their local authors/creators.

SELF-/MICROPUBLISHING SERVICES

There are dozens of services and tools to support self-publishing authors. Below, we focus on full-service publishing and distribution platforms and highlight some additional tools for more tech-savvy authors.

Self-Publishing Platforms

- *Scribd* (http://www.scribd.com/upload-document) helps authors publish content on the web and on mobile devices and helps them distribute and sell their content to a global audience.
- *Lulu* (http://www.lulu.com/) is a self-publishing platform for print, e-books, photo books, calendars, and more.
- *BookBaby* (http://www.bookbaby.com/) is another all-in-one self-print/e-book publishing platform, with basic free services and a full suite of add-ons, including editing help.
- *Smashwords* (http://www.smashwords.com/) is primarily an e-book distribution platform, with tools for marketing, distribution, metadata management, and sales reporting.
- *Issuu* (http://issuu.com/) is a fast-growing digital publishing platform tailored to visual works like magazines and photo-illustrated books on topics such as fashion, lifestyle, art, sports, and global affairs.
- *Amazon self-publishing services.* Amazon offers three specialized self-publishing platforms:
  - Kindle Direct Publishing (https://kdp.amazon.com)
  - Create Space for print and non-Kindle e-books (https://www.create space.com/)
  - Audiobook Creation Exchange (ACX) for audiobooks (http://www.acx .com/)
- *iBooks Author* (http://www.apple.com/ibooks-author/) is an Apple app that enables authors to create enhanced e-books designed specifically for iPads and Macs. The enhanced e-books can include elements such as photo galleries, video, interactive diagrams, 3-D objects, and more.
- *IngramSpark* (http://www1.ingramspark.com/) is another full-service publishing platform with the additional advantage that it's part of Ingram, making distribution to libraries easier.

Highlighted Tools

- *Pressbooks* (http://pressbooks.com/) is an online tool to convert finished manuscripts into e-books or POD-ready files. It is free for basic use, or Pressbooks will do it for you for a fee.
- *Inkscape* (http://www.inkscape.org/en/) is an open-source vector graphics tool used to design high-quality cover art (figure 2.2).
- *BiblioCrunch* (http://bibliocrunch.com/) is a service to connect authors and publishers with book publishing professionals in order to get new books and apps to market.

Figure 2.2. Inkscape, a free online tool to design cover art.

- *Vook* (http://vook.com), formerly an e-book sales data service for traditional publishers, is now opening up to self-publishing authors on a limited basis.

Adding Audio, the Next Big Thing?

Digital audiobooks, like e-books, have been around for a long time, but now it's possible to include read-along narration in enhanced e-books both on mobile devices and on standalone platforms. These features have been available as accessibility tools and for children's books but seem to have hit a tipping point as part of mainstream adult e-books.

- *TumbleBooks* (http://tumbleBookcloud.com/) and its collection of digital children's books have been used by libraries for years, and both Tumble-Books and TumbleBookCloud (for older students and low-literacy adults) offer read-along narration for many items.
- *Kindle Unlimited Audiobooks with Whispersync for Voice* (http://www.amazon.com/b?node=9578129011). The Kindle Unlimited subscription service allows access to "over 700,000 titles and thousands of audiobooks" via the Kindle's passive Whispernet updating system.[1]

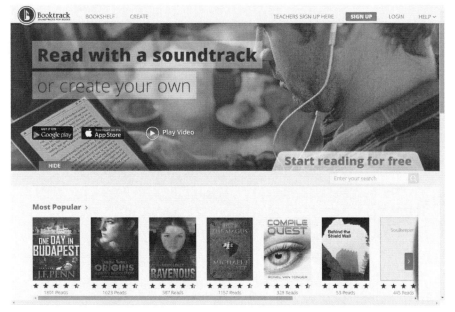

Figure 2.3.   Tools such as BookTrack give creators interactive ways to offer their works online.

- *Audiobook Creation Exchange* (ACX) from Audible/Amazon (http://www .acx.com/) is a marketplace connecting authors and publishers with independent audiobook narrators and engineers.
- *BookTrack* (http://www.booktrack.com) enables authors to upload their book and add a soundtrack of music, narration, or effects to play along while someone reads online (figure 2.3).

Library-Specific Tools

- *indieBRAG* (http://www.bragmedallion.com/) is a review and vetting site for independent, self-published e-books. Contributors are well-read individuals and book club members (aka, "real readers").
- *BiblioBoard* (http://biblioboard.com/libraries/index.html) is a service for libraries to provide simultaneous online reading to their users, offering e-books with no wait lists or hold limits.
- *SELF-E* from BiblioBoard (http://biblioboard.com/SELF-e/), powered by *Library Journal*, allows public libraries to take submissions from local self-published authors and make the e-books available to users through the BiblioBoard platform (figure 2.4).
- *Espresso Book Machine* (EBM) from OnDemand Books (http://www .ondemandbooks.com/) is an all-in-one print-on-demand machine—a

Figure 2.4. The Los Gatos Public Library system is one of many libraries using the SELF-E platform to support local self-published authors.

high-speed photocopier tied to a paperback binding machine—producing library-quality paperbacks in minutes. Initially popular in bookstores and academic libraries, more public libraries are investing in these machines in order to support self-publishing.

LIBRARY APPLICATIONS

Libraries can get involved in self-publishing at many levels and in many different ways. Walt Crawford sums it up nicely in *The Librarian's Guide to Micropublishing*:

> Public libraries service lifelong learning, and serve to collect, organize, and preserve the stories that make up our civilization. Micropublishing adds new local voices to that set of stories. . . . Public libraries already gather the resources to make micropublishing work well and to benefit from its possibilities. . . . Who better than the library to facilitate [this] process?[2]

How much support your library can give to local/self-published creators is only limited by your imagination, the needs of your community, and your resources. Some ideas, based on what libraries are already doing, include:

- Purchase self-published materials and invite local self-published authors to speak.
- Highlight reader services like Smashwords and Issuu on the library website, especially any local authors or locally relevant books.

- Provide lists of resources local creators (authors, designers, illustrators, editors) can use to find each other or provide a venue for these creators to gather and work together.
- Offer workshops on self-publishing, e-book publishing, creative writing, copyediting, or book illustration and cover design. Alternately, promote and provide computer time for creators to take online courses on self-publishing techniques and tools.
- Provide computers, printers, photocopiers, and other technology self-publishers can use to create their works.
- Collaborate with local colleges and universities to offer low-cost or free creative writing or publishing courses.
- Find a space for a dedicated writing/self-publishing center with the technology and staff to support it.
- Invest in an Espresso Book Machine, e-book publishing platform, or other technology to turn your library into a community publisher.
- Create a library publishing imprint that provides a complete service for local authors.

Crawford's *The Librarian's Guide to Micropublishing* is the single best resource for libraries interested in supporting local self-publishing authors, walking you through every step in the self-publishing process and suggesting best practices and possible vendors.

LIBRARY PROGRAMS SUPPORTING SELF-/ MICROPUBLISHING

Many libraries currently offer programs and events that support self-publishing authors. Below are a few examples of these types of programs.

Seattle Writes (http://www.spl.org/audiences/adults/seattle-writes), Seattle Public Library, Seattle, WA

Seattle Writes is a project to support local authors and connect them with our large and avid community of readers. It includes workshops on the craft of writing, write-ins, author panels, classes on digital publishing and more.[3]

The Wire: A Writer's Resource (http://blogs.douglascountylibraries .org/thewire/, Douglas County Public Libraries, Denver, CO

The Wire: A Writer's Resource from Douglas County Public Libraries (Denver, CO) grew out of the Denver County Model for expanding the ways public libraries buy materials, including print and e-books.

"Writing Workshop: Self-Publishing Your eBook" (http://www.indianaauthorsaward.org/upcoming-events/writing-workshop-self-publishing-eBook/), Indianapolis Public Library, Indianapolis, IN

"Writing Workshop: Self-Publishing Your eBook" was a series of self-publishing workshops held at Indianapolis Public Library (IN) branches in conjunction with the Indy Author Fair, the Eugene and Marilyn Glick Indiana Authors Award, and the Indiana Writers Center.

"How Do I Self-Publish an eBook?" (http://www.wellfleetlibrary.org/index.php/seminars-classes-and-workshops/event/2315-eBook-publishing), Wellfleet Public Library, Wellfleet, MA

As part of a series at the Wellfleet Public Library, local author Laura Shabott presented "How Do I Self-Publish an eBook?" and discussed her experiences with other potential authors (http://www.wellfleetlibrary.org/index.php/seminars-classes-and-workshops/event/2315-eBook-publishing). Shabott is the author of *Confessions of an eBook Virgin: What Everyone Should Know before They Publish on the Internet*, published by Provincetown Public Press (see "Library as Publisher" under "Library Examples" below).

"Ebook Publishing in the Classroom" (http://blog.smashwords.com/2014/05/ebook-publishing-in-classroom-los-gatos.html), Smashwords and Los Gatos Public Library, CA

Smashwords CEO Mark Coker has been collaborating with Los Gatos Public Library (CA) director Henry Bankhead for several years on ways to bring together self-publishing companies and libraries, including a pilot program consisting of three educational workshops at the library to help library staff and local writers learn how to e-publish like professionals followed by a grant-funded project to bring a mobile self-publishing workshop to the local high school. According to Coker:

> Public libraries provide an essential community service by promoting literacy and a culture of reading. Now, libraries have an exciting opportunity to help promote a culture of authorship in their communities. Libraries are uniquely qualified to marshal community resources and talent to help local writers become professional publishers. Local self-published authors, in turn, have an opportunity—working with the library—to give back to their community by mentoring the next generation of writers. By sponsoring educational seminars and events, libraries can bring local authors face-to-face with readers and writers. Libraries can help unleash the talent locked inside the minds and fingertips of their community's writers.[4]

LIBRARY EXAMPLES

Supporting Self-/Micropublishing through Programs and Print on Demand

The Sacramento Public Library (SPL) was one of the first public libraries in the United States to buy an Espresso Book Machine (EBM) for use by the general public. At the same time, SPL teamed up with a community college that was eliminating its creative writing program in order to offer those same classes at the library. These two projects were combined into I Street Press, a staff-supported service for self-publishing authors (http://www.saclibrary .org/istreet/). Through I Street Press, creators can learn how to prepare their manuscripts to be printed on the EBM and receive personalized help with the process, for a reasonable fee (figure 2.5). Coordinator Gerald Ward describes the program this way:

> I Street Press is a service offered by the Sacramento Public Library for the people of Sacramento and surrounding areas. We have printed books for people and organizations from Los Angeles, CA, and Denver, CO. Authors contact the I Street Press and attend an Information Session held twice a month. The Information Sessions explain the process, what we can do for the authors and what the author needs to do to be successful. These sessions include levels of service,

Figure 2.5. Paul Reaves, author of *The Truth! What Color Is Your Soul?* published his work with the support of I Street Press at Sacramento Public Library. Sacramento Public Library, used with permission.

pricing, expectations and limitations. We are already successful. After three years of offering this service, I Street Press has published more than 11,500 books and 185 titles from more than 140 authors. We use an OnDemand Books Espresso Book Making Machine on-site to enable authors to watch their books being printed. Hundreds of people have come to information sessions, seen the press at work while on tours and have had individual appointments, with 90% of those appointments resulting in a finished book.[5]

As of early 2015, six public libraries had EBMs and offered staff support and some programs and events that introduce the basics of printing with the EBM and how to get the most out of self-publishing for print.

- Sacramento Public Library (Sacramento, CA)—main library
- Mid-Continent Public Library (Kansas City, MO)—Woodneath Library Center
- District of Columbia Public Library (Washington, DC)—Digital Commons at Martin Luther King Jr. Memorial Library, Central Library
- Windsor Public Library (Ontario, Canada)—X-Press Self-Publishing Lab, Central Library
- Edmonton Public Library (Edmonton, Canada)—EPL Makerspace at the Stanley A. Milner Public Library
- Loudoun County Public Library (VA)—Symington Press at the Rust Library, Leesburg, VA

See which libraries currently have EBMs at http://www.ondemandbooks .com/ebm_locations_list.php.

Library as Publisher

In 2012, the Provincetown Public Library (MA) created an enriched e-book about the library to support a service award application. The Provincetown staff were so pleased with the process and the result that they decided to offer local writers and authors the opportunity to publish e-books by establishing the Provincetown Public Press. Using the skills they learned while creating their own book, press staff were able to support authors (selected by a committee) through the entire process of creating an e-book, including editing, layout, and copyright acquisition. The finished books are submitted for distribution under the Provincetown Public Press imprint, although authors are still responsible for their own marketing.

"In 2013, the Provincetown Public Press published a total of 5 books, 4 of which were completely original releases," says Matt Clark, director of marketing and program development of the Provincetown Public Library. "The books were released to the Apple iBook store and Amazon on November 1, 2013. The collective launch date was celebrated at an event at the Library on November 14, 2013, featuring all of our authors. In 2014, the Press Published one additional book entitled *Love on the Beat*, an art book focused on Terry Catalano's photographs of Parisian collective graffiti. The release of the book was accompanied by a two-day interactive art exhibit. 2014 also saw the Press turn its focus to consistently releasing community-created content [and] the release of *Sustenance* (http://readsustenance.com), an online magazine celebrating the creative spirit of the Outer Cape. The site published two new releases each week from May 1 to October 1, and we are currently collecting and creating content for our 2015 season."[6]

After hearing about Provincetown's success, Director Dolores Greenwald of the Williamson County Public Library (TN) reached out to neighboring business Ingram Books to see if the library could offer their local authors a similar service. Supported by excited staff and the IngramSpark platform, Williamson County launched the Janice Keck Literary Awards and Academy Park Press in 2013 (figure 2.6).

> The Williamson County Public Library has published two books under its publishing imprint Academy Park Press. The Library assists local authors in numerous ways in order for them to publish and gain recognition in our community. This year, the Williamson County Library launched the first The Janice Keck Literary Awards selecting outstanding writing in four different categories: adult fiction, adult non-fiction, poetry, and children's literature. There were forty-seven entries! The Library awards the winners an IngramSpark account, ISBN number and ten copies of their work. This will be an annual event as the Library moves forward to work with local writers in exciting and unique ways.[7]

Both Provincetown Public Press and Academy Park Press offer many of the services of a traditional publisher: editorial and formatting assistance, preparation for publication, copyright and ISBN acquisition, and basic advice on

Figure 2.6. Winning authors from Williamson County Public Library, published through Academy Park Press. Williamson County Public Library, used with permission.

distribution and marketing. Authors are responsible for any further promotion of their work.

No matter which technologies they use or how they get started, it's easier than ever before for authors, photographers, illustrators, and artists to share their work with a global audience. Libraries can continue to contribute to this growing culture of independent creators through any of the programs discussed here and in ways yet to be discovered.

NOTES

1. Amazon, "Introducing Kindle Unlimited," Amazon: Kindle Unlimited, accessed February 25, 2015, http://www.amazon.com/b?node=9578129011.

2. Walt Crawford, *The Librarian's Guide to Micropublishing: Helping Patrons and Communities Use Free and Low-Cost Publishing Tools to Tell Their Stories* (Medford, NJ: Information Today, 2012), 5.

3. "Seattle Writes," Seattle Public Library, accessed February 25, 2015, http://www.spl.org/audiences/adults/seattle-writes.

4. Mark Coker, "How Libraries Can Launch Community Publishing Initiatives with Self-Published Ebooks," *Smashwords* (blog), March 23, 2013, accessed February 25, 2015, http://blog.smashwords.com/2013/03/how-libraries-can-launch-community.html.

5. Gerald Ward, "Local Authors Find a Voice at the Library," Knight News Challenge, accessed February 25, 2015, https://www.newschallenge.org/challenge/libraries/feedback/local-authors-find-a-voice-at-the-library.

6. E-mail response from Matt Clark, 11/10/2014.

7. E-mail response from Dolores Greenwald, 11/7/2014.

Chapter Three

Mobile Technologies

WHAT'S EMERGING ABOUT MOBILE TECHNOLOGIES?

As with audio and video, mobile devices are older technologies being reinvented with current innovations and "emerging" all over again. In this chapter, we define a mobile device as any handheld wireless device capable of two-way communication. Currently, these include

- mobile phones (feature phones);
- smartphones;
- tablets and other handheld computers;
- personal game and media players, including web-enabled e-readers; and
- older technologies like personal digital assistants (PDAs), pagers, Wi-Fi digital cameras, and so on (figure 3.1).

Today's high-powered handheld computers and high-speed cellular and Wi-Fi networks allow for constant connection and immediate access to information. More importantly, these tools are increasingly ubiquitous. According to the Pew Research Center's Internet and American Life Project,[1] as of January 2014:

- 90% of American adults have a cell phone
- 58% of American adults have a smartphone
- 32% of American adults own an e-reader
- 42% of American adults own a tablet computer

What this means for libraries is that most library users are likely to have a cellphone and more than half of those are app-capable smartphones. Support

Figure 3.1.   Mobile devices are an integral part of our users' lives. Jeremy Keith via Wikimedia Commons.

for mobile technology has become an expected part of library service, just like e-books and an online catalog. Mobile devices tend to cost less than laptops or desktop computers and come with their own Internet connections (via cellular data or Wi-Fi). Someone who cannot afford, or has nowhere to keep, a larger computer can own an inexpensive smartphone with a monthly minutes plan and be just as connected to the online world. Or patrons may only own an e-reader with basic, if any, web surfing capabilities and no ability to use apps. Libraries need to provide all patrons with services equitable to those offered to more tech-savvy users.

Recent advances in mobile technologies will help expand services and make existing services easier to maintain, beginning with the mobile interface. Until recently, there were two ways for a third party to interact with a mobile user: via a mobile website or through an app. However, developing a mobile website means maintaining duplicate content or using advanced website code, and not every library has the ability to create an app. Responsive web design, developed in the early 2010s, allows a single site to serve screens of all sizes (figure 3.2). Information from the browser on a device tells the site how big the available screen is, and the settings on the site show more or less detail as appropriate. On small screens, images, extra links, interactive

Figure 3.2. Responsive design displays well on any size screen.

elements, and other screen real estate hogs are hidden, and only the most important menu items remain. Responsive web design makes it much easier to use a single interface for all user devices and eliminates the need to maintain either a separate site or a stand-alone app.

In hardware, the most interesting trends in mobile computing include near-field communication/mobile payment; non-phone mobile devices such as smartwatches; and tiny computers embedded in ordinary things like photo frames, light bulbs, medical devices, and even clothing. Smartwatches and the embedded computers will both be discussed separately in chapter 5 ("Wearables") and chapter 6 ("The Internet of Things").

Near-field communication (NFC) has been around for more than a decade but has only recently found uses in mobile technology. In NFC, a low-powered microchip in a card or device makes a radio connection with another chip in very close range—usually touching—and exchanges information, such as a credit card payment transaction. For example, using a service like Google Wallet (http://www.google.com/wallet/) or Apple Pay (http://www.apple.com/apple-pay/), the mobile phone transmits payment information to a store's NFC reader, allowing you to pay without ever directly risking your credit card information (figure 3.3).

Figure 3.3. "An hour of magical parking": NFC payment at a parking meter. Jason Tester Guerilla Future (Flickr user: streamishmc) via Wikimedia Commons.

PROS AND CONS

The question is no longer *whether* libraries need to provide mobile-friendly services but rather *which* services should be provided and how they should be offered and supported. There are no "right" answers to the following questions; every library needs determine what's right for its own situation and users.

What Kind of Mobile Interface?
Mobile Website versus Library App

Both mobile-friendly websites and apps can offer a robust experience for library mobile users, so it's a matter of which suits a library and its patrons better. Library apps need to be discovered and downloaded by patrons before they can be used, each operating system needs an individually developed app, and the apps need to be separately maintained and updated with fixes and improvements as the operating system of the devices upgrade. However, small libraries and libraries that are part of a larger municipal or county system may not have a choice in the design of their website, so an app would give them the autonomy to provide mobile services without relying on the website to do so.

Nowadays, rather than develop a separate mobile website, a library could use responsive design for the primary website, which would provide mobile users with integrated access to all of the library's resources. Also, using responsive design means current library information needs to be updated in only one place instead of on both an app and a website. The downside is that not all libraries may be ready to redesign their website with responsive design, and a website overhaul is a major undertaking that requires much planning.

Who Creates and Maintains the Interface?

Asking library staff to create and maintain an app or a website means that updates are immediate, and the overall cost may be lower if your library has skilled staff able to do this work. Using a vendor outsources the work and as a result may cost more; it also removes some control over changes and how the site or app works behind the scenes.

How Will the Library Site/App Connect to Any Third-Party Vendors—e-books, Databases, Streaming Media, and More?

The issues here are the number of devices/operating systems supported by the vendor apps or sites and how much or little control a library has over how patrons are being asked to work with these resources.

Who Is the Library Serving with Mobile Services, How Do They Access Those Services, and What Services Should/Can Be Offered?

When a library offers mobile services, it also needs to provide guidance to help its users navigate those services. Classes, drop-in "petting zoos," in-person and online help, and other programs are all needed to support the services offered. Just like librarians used to teach people how to use the card catalog or the shelving systems, now we must show our patrons how to download and open e-books, troubleshoot their media players, and install our apps. The advantages of this are better-served patrons and more used services, while the challenges include staff skill gaps and overstretched staff time.

A major consideration for all libraries offering mobile services is the increasing digital divide—the widening gap between what the most tech-savvy and economically advantaged users have access to versus patrons with less money to spend on gadgets and less ability to use them. Libraries, particularly public libraries, must serve all of these users as equitably as possible. Offering e-books that can only be read on a Kindle or Nook, subscribing to streaming media that isn't playable on less-advanced but still commonly used smartphones, or only offering apps on a single operating system (usually iOS), cuts off library patrons from services just because they lack the technology to use them. Even making the library's website unreachable by anyone without a strong Internet connection (through the use of complex code or numerous images) widens the digital divide, though in this last case, a mobile-friendly responsive site solves that problem by allowing browsers to choose what they display (figure 3.4).

Another way to shrink the digital divide is to provide devices for patron checkout and use. For this, the pros and cons are more obvious: lending technology to patrons invites damage and loss, may inspire inappropriate use by patrons, requires maintenance and replacement of the devices, and can have a very high overall cost to the library. However, there is no easier way to make sure that a patron has access to mobile library resources than to simply lend them a device.

MOBILE TECHNOLOGY AND SERVICES

There are two aspects to mobile technology: the physical devices and the interfaces on them that make them useful.

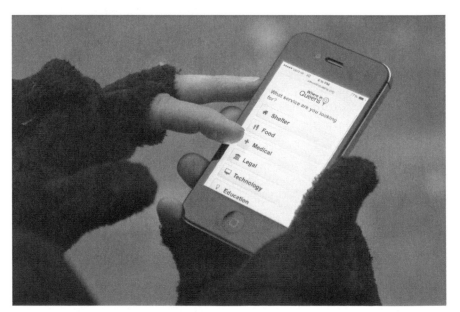

Figure 3.4.   WhereInQueens.org was designed to display best on inexpensive smartphones in order to be accessible by any device.

Hardware

The hardware involved in mobile services largely consists of your patrons' own devices, unless your library has chosen to lend devices directly. A quick review of major manufacturers of mobile devices includes

- Apple—iPhone (smartphone), iPad (tablet), iPhone 6 Plus (phablet), iPod (media player and mini-tablet);
- Samsung, LG, Motorola, HTC, Sony Mobile, Nokia, and so on—devices running the Android and Windows Phone platforms;
- Amazon—Kindle Fire (e-reader/basic tablet);
- Nook (e-reader/basic tablet); and
- Sony, Nintendo, and others—mobile gaming devices with basic web browsers.

However, if libraries adopt NFC for library cards, payments, or "dumber" chips that offer book recommendations or details about library services, they would need to purchase NFC readers and chip technology to enable these services.

Interfaces

There are three primary ways for a user to interact with his or her mobile device:

- *Native/basic interface:* the interfaces that come with the device (i.e., operating system, keyboard, keypad, buttons, touch screens, menus, settings, etc.)
- *Apps:* software applications developed by the device maker and third-party companies to allow users to achieve specific tasks with their device; each one is unique, but they share many similar features
- *Mobile web:* a web browser on the device, using Wi-Fi to connect to the Internet

Native Interfaces

Currently, the three major operating systems are iOS (Apple devices), Android (most other devices), and Windows Phone (Windows devices). The native interface for each of these is very different, and many libraries offer workshops and classes for their patrons on how to use the basic features of their smartphone or tablet.

Apps

In addition to their own library app (for catalogs, circulation/account interactions, and general library information), other types of apps most likely to be used with library services can include

- library vendor apps (Overdrive, Zinio, Hoopla, 3M Cloud Library eBooks);
- database apps (EbscoHost Mobile, AccessMyLibrary from Gale Cengage);
- e-book apps (Kindle app, Stanza, iBooks, Nook app, Fictionwise eReader [Project Gutenberg], Classics app [a short list of "classic" free e-books]);
- reference apps, including science, anatomy, math, spelling, dictionary/thesaurus, encyclopedia, history, grammar, art, music, and more;
- literature and reader's advisory apps (GoodReads, LibraryThing, Novelist, WorldCat Mobile, BookMyne from SirsiDynix, Bibliocommons);
- language-learning apps (Duolingo, Mango Languages, Rosetta Stone);
- productivity apps (Dropbox; Google Drive; Evernote; MS OneNote; If This, Then That);
- camera and photo-editing apps (native camera apps, PhotoSphere, Lightroom, Photoshop, Snapseed, PicTapGo, Camera+);
- augmented-reality apps (Layar, Yelp Monocle, SpyGlass, Google SkyMap);
- games, especially educational games for kids; and
- social media apps (Facebook, Pinterest, Instagram, Twitter, Tumblr, Reddit, and many more).

Another service that a library can provide is to recommend and teach specific apps to its patrons. A quick search online for "recommended apps for libraries" will bring up hundreds of results, or see chapter 8, "Keeping Up with Emerging Technologies," for ways to stay on top of the latest offerings and hottest new trends in apps.

Mobile Web

As previously discussed, the best investment that a library can make in serving mobile users via its website is to redesign the site using responsive design. A mobile patron can open a browser, navigate to the library's website, and use it on any size screen with minimal fuss. The user will have access to all of the library's services, and it's much easier for the library to maintain that single resource.

Library App or Mobile Site Development

If your library wants to hire a vendor to develop or redesign a library app or mobile website, you can either contract with a small local company (just search the white pages for "web developer"), or find a library-specific vendor.

If you decide to develop and maintain an app in-house, you'll need to work with the development platforms for each mobile operating system you want to offer an app for. Look for information for developers and the software development kit (SDK) for iOS, Android, and Windows Phone.

If you choose to go with a mobile-friendly or mobile-first site and want to do it yourself, you'll either need developers on staff to create and maintain that site or you can use a content management system (CMS) that has responsive design built into the theme. CMSs make it easy to maintain a site in general, and many CMS themes include responsive design elements by default, so no additional coding is needed.

App and CMS Vendors

- *Boopsie* (http://www.boopsie.com). Boopsie was one of the first and remains the largest developer for library apps. Boopsie apps combine in-app content with links back to the library website for services such as online fine payments and some database use (figure 3.5).
- *LibGuides CMS* (http://www.springshare.com/libguides/cms.html). Springshare developed LibGuides to offer online research and topic guides

Figure 3.5. A Boopsie library app interface for mobile devices.

to academic and special libraries. Springshare now offers LibGuides CMS, which libraries can use to create a responsively designed library website that integrates all of Springshare's LibApps services seamlessly.

- *Bibliocommons* (http://www.bibliocommons.com/products/cms and http://www.bibliocommons.com/products/mobile). Originally a discovery layer designed to work with a library's existing catalog system, the Bibliocommons platform has evolved into a web content platform in its own right. BiblioCMS offers a content management system for a library's responsively designed website, while BiblioMobile is a standalone app platform.
- *Other CMS platforms.* Wordpress (http://www.wordpress.com), Joomla (http://www.joomla.org), Drupal (http://www.drupal.org), and other well-known content management systems all offer layout themes that include responsive design. If your library already uses a content management system, it's a matter of finding the right theme that supports what you want to do.

LIBRARY APPLICATIONS

Mobile Library Services

As we've seen, one of the easiest ways to offer mobile services is by making the library's website and catalog easily available via a mobile device. Another is by offering mobile reference, usually through an interaction like "Text your question and we'll get back to you with an answer or a link." In the future, mobile collaboration tools like Talko (http://www.talko.com) and Quip (http://quip.com) could enable mobile-based reference to be a robust and fully interactive service. Quip allows multiple users to create and edit a collaborative document, including any related discussion via text, chat, and notes. Talko takes this one step further by including voice memos and live phone calls as part of the collaborative document.[2] Imagine a library reference service based on either of these tools and how well it could re-create an in-person reference/reader's advisory transaction with the convenience of remote access.

Paying Fines and Fees

Many libraries are already offering their patrons the ability to scan their library cards into loyalty card apps like CardStar (http://www.cardstar.com/) and KeyRing (http://www.keyringapp.com). The next possible step is to allow direct mobile payments in one of two ways: in-app on a library app or using NFC technology. To date, we haven't found any libraries using in-app payments; even the largest library mobile app developer, Boopsie, will point app users to a library's traditional online payment page instead of offering the ability to pay fines and fees from directly within the app. Developing in-app payments would make library apps truly a library-in-a-pocket, though the continued development of responsive websites might be as useful.

Similarly, while NFC technology currently is used in libraries in a limited way, the growing availability of NFC payment options may be implemented in libraries in the future. NFC readers at checkout counters and kiosks would allow patrons to pay directly with their smartphones through services like Apple Pay and Google Wallet.

Accessing Collections

For years, libraries have been using mobile-friendly webpage URLs, QR codes, and RFID tags on posters, on stack labels, and on materials themselves to create connections between the physical library and online services. A mobile-friendly access point might connect to an item's catalog record, to information about a program, or to relevant sections of the library's website. Improvements in library apps and technology like NFC tags will make it easier to enhance the physical environment of the library via mobile devices.

Augmented reality (AR) in libraries via smart devices has been slow to catch on, largely due to the complexity of creating AR content. Some libraries are successfully using AR apps such as Layar (http://www.layar.com/) and homegrown applications to add to the experience of being in a library building, usually working with outside companies or local colleges to provide the technical expertise. Using resources from digital collections and information about the library—often links back to the library catalog—patrons can turn on the Layar app, point it at different areas of the library, and get overlays of information right on their mobile screen.

Another possible way for patrons to interact with library collections via their mobile devices could involve "gadgets" like the new Google Cardboard (figure 3.6), a do-it-yourself virtual reality attachment for Android devices (an iOS version was released later in 2014). According to the product website, Cardboard is "a no-frills enclosure that transforms a phone into a basic VR headset, and the accompanying open software toolkit that makes writing VR software as simple as building a web or mobile app."[3] If a phone has panoramic pictures or PhotoSphere full-surround images, viewing them with the Cardboard attachment adds a 3-D effect and allows you to turn your body to see everything "around" you. Imagine viewing a digital collection of stereoscope images, pictures of 3-D objects in library collections, or

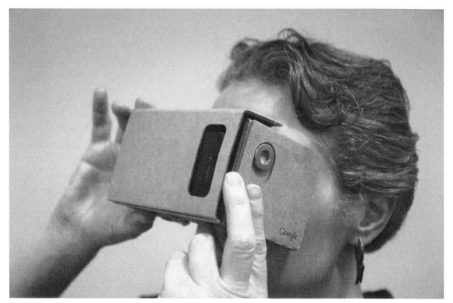

Figure 3.6. Google Cardboard can bring interactive virtual elements to any library for a reasonable cost.

up-close views of fragile library materials through an inexpensive virtual reality headset. A library could purchase a few low-cost mobile devices and enough $20 Cardboard kits to match, then check out the virtual reality collection for in-library use.

If you're interested in building something into a full 3-D experience, take a look at our discussion of Oculus Rift in chapter 5, "Wearables."

LIBRARY EXAMPLES

Services

Libraries such as the Des Plaines Public Library (IL) have simple instructions for how patrons can scan their library cards into loyalty card apps like CardStar and KeyRing or even directly into Google Wallet. Patrons scan their cards and use their smartphones instead of plastic.[4]

At the Pasadena County Library (CA), librarians have developed a comprehensive Appvisory program to help parents and caregivers understand apps and find the best ones to use with their children. It is a combination of an app-based eStorytime, an afterschool Appy Hour to teach device literacy and offer free play to students, iPad stations in the children's room preloaded with selected apps, and an online presence for parents and caregivers offering lists of best apps for kids.[5]

Devices

In October of 2012, Superstorm Sandy flooded much of the New York City borough of Queens. Many residents lost everything, and the Queens Public Library (PL) stepped in to help provide information and resources. Working with Governor Andrew Cuomo and New York state offices, Google donated five thousand Google Nexus Tablets to Queens Library for use in affected areas; however, most broadband and cell phone infrastructure was destroyed, reducing the tablets' functionality. Under the leadership of Kelvin Watson (vice president of digital services) and Lisa Epps (vice president of information technology/CIO), Queens PL built a customized tablet platform preloaded with content that can be used entirely offline and updated and expanded when connected to Wi-Fi. The clean, icon-driven interface provides a "guided experience" on select topics (education, job-search information, healthcare resources, information for new Americans), apps for library resources like e-books (Overdrive and Blio), and magazine-style hyper-local information. As Watson and Epps write in a forthcoming case study: "The tablet interface makes it friendly to even the most tech-resistant customer. There is no intimidating external keyboard. There are no parts to break. All the customer needs to do is poke at it to discover useful information. The more they experiment, the more likely they are to play with it. Perceived barriers are eroded and customers gain a measure of digital literacy."[6] Queens PL also worked with a software management vendor to customize a remote maintenance system that lets staff quickly reset a device when it's returned, deleting patron information and allowing tablets to be loaned out "clean." Tablets are loaned for one month, with up to three renewals. In the first ten months of the program, Queens Public Library lent devices to 2,700 users through eight library locations and an average of forty devices per week at the central library (figure 3.7). The next step is to lend the devices throughout the borough so that all library users can benefit.[7]

Apps and Mobile Websites

More recently, Queens PL staff helped develop WhereinQueens.org (http://www.whereinqueens.org/), a mobile site designed to serve low-income and homeless populations who have bought or been given low-cost smartphones. In spring of 2014, the Tenderloin Technology Lab in San Francisco presented at South by Southwest Interactive on Link-SF, "a mobile-optimized platform

Figure 3.7. Students use the circulating tablets at the Queens Public Library. Queens Public Library, used with permission.

that connects its users with basic services (food, shelter, hygiene, medical care, and technology access) around them."[8] After listening to this talk and realizing that many homeless patrons in Queens also have smartphones, Lauren Comito (job and business academy manager at Queens PL) worked with five interns over the summer to develop a similar platform for Queens based on the code from Link-SF. WhereinQueens.org launched in September of 2014, and Comito is working with homeless shelters and other organizations to spread the word. "We help people find jobs, and overcome the barriers to doing so. If you don't have a place to sleep or take a bath, it's hard to get and keep a job. We wanted to build this to help them get past the barriers."[9] Their next steps are to get WhereinQueens.org added to the circulating tablet platform and expand the site's reach.

The Boston Public Library is about to release a mobile website–based video tour of some of the murals in the historic McKim Building.

After 119 years of inviting the public into the building to use the library and enjoy its art and architectural treasures, our forms of interpretation are still evolving. We have a vibrant volunteer art and architecture tour guide program, but wanted to offer patrons a chance to receive a "tour" of these spaces when a guide is not present. The process of building a smart phone tour began several years ago, and we are finally revisiting the project, starting with a tour of our three major mural cycles. We have found through early testing that patrons want options as to how they engage with the technology. Sometimes there's a desire for a quick reference (e.g., "what's happening in this panel"), for which we have built in room elevations with hotspots that the patron can select. Others might want to explore the piece in depth, so we have been able to offer them a brief (approx. 3-minute) video that gives a more formal audio/visual tour of the space. The best practice for evaluating the project has been testing on-site and asking users for feedback. A huge advantage of this app is that it can be readily changed and improved![10]

At the Los Angeles Public Library, digital journalism professor Robert Hernandez of the University of Southern California (USC) Annenberg School for Communication and Journalism worked with the library to "augment" the historic Central Library building. Over the course of a semester in 2013, students in Hernandez's augmented-reality storytelling and journalism course created an app that overlays the library's art, architecture, and collections with visual, video, and 3-D experiences. The app is now available for all visitors to the main library (https://itunes.apple.com/us/app/archive-lapl/id821138097?mt=8).

The National Library Board of Singapore recently introduced a new mobile app that has all of the expected features of a mobile app but also allows in-app checkouts of materials by scanning the library barcode.[11]

NFC

In 2013, the library of Saitama Prefecture in Hanno, Japan, installed NFC tags from Fuji that allow patrons to see a list of books usually on that shelf that are currently checked out (and place reserves on them), link to more information about titles and authors, and access the library's catalog.[12]

NOTES

1. Pew Research Center, Internet and American Life Project, "Mobile Technology Fact Sheet," Fact Sheets, http://www.pewinternet.org/fact-sheets/mobile-technology -fact-sheet/.

2. Details about Talko and Quip are from https://medium.com/@stevenlevy/ brave-new-phone-call-f4064a4e720 and Ted Greenwald, "Mobil Collaboration: The Smartphone Era Is Finally Getting the Productivity Software It Needs," *MIT Technology Review*, http://www.technologyreview.com/featuredstory/526526/mobile -collaboration/.

3. Google, "Cardboard," Get Cardboard, http://cardboard.withgoogle.com/.

4. Roberta Johnson, "Scan Your Card," Patron Services, Des Plaines Public Library, accessed February 26, 2015, http://dppl.org/patron-services/scan-your-card.

5. Carolyn Sun, "Appvisory for Educational Children's Apps," The Digital Shift, October 3, 2014, accessed February 26, 2015, http://www.thedigitalshift.com/2014/10/k-12/appvisory-educational-apps-tds14/.

6. Lisa Epps and Kelvin Watson, "Library of the Future: Emergency! How Queens Library Came to the Rescue with Info Resources after Hurricane Sandy," *Computers in Libraries* (forthcoming).

7. American Library Association, "Queens Library Wins the ALA/Information Today, Inc. Library of the Future Award," ALA News, April 22, 2014, accessed February 2, 2015, http://www.ala.org/news/press-releases/2014/04/queens-library-wins-alainformation-today-inc-library-future-award.

8. South by Southwest 2014 Schedule, "Mobile Technology Solutions for the Marginalized," accessed February 26, 2015, http://schedule.sxsw.com/2014/events/event_IAP17184.

9. Phone interview with Lauren Comito, 11/14/2014.

10. E-mail response from Meghan Weeks, exhibitions and outreach associate, Boston Public Library, 11/12/2014.

11. National Library Board, "Upgrade Your Library Experience with myLibrary!" News and Announcements, National Library Board Singapore, September 19, 2014, accessed February 26, 2015, http://www.nlb.gov.sg/NewsAnnouncement/tabid/225/announcementId/76/Default.aspx#.VDIRVucoz9q.

12. Shayne Rana, "Japan's First NFC Equipped Library Lets You Rate, Review and Comment on Books with a Simple Tap of the Phone," *New Launches*, accessed February 26, 2015, http://newlaunches.com/archives/japans-first-nfc-equipped-library-lets-you-rate-review-and-comment-on-books-with-a-simple-tap-of-the-phone.php.

Chapter Four

Crowdfunding

WHAT IS CROWDFUNDING?

In these days of tight library budgets, sometimes you have a great idea but you don't have the funds to implement it. If you find yourself in this situation, you may want to consider trying to crowdfund your idea. According to *Wikipedia*:

> Crowdfunding is the practice of funding a project or venture by raising monetary contributions from a large number of people, typically via the Internet. One early-stage equity expert described it as "the practice of raising funds from two or more people over the internet towards a common Service, Project, Product, Investment, Cause, and Experience." The crowdfunding model is fueled by three types of actors: the project initiator who proposes the idea and/or project to be funded; individuals or groups who support the idea; and a moderating organization (the "platform") that brings the parties together to launch the idea.[1]

Simply put, you have an idea and you ask others to contribute funds to make that idea come to fruition. While crowdfunding isn't a technology itself, it uses the technology of the Internet to broaden your funding base and is still relatively new to libraries. Generally, the crowdfunding process works like this:

1. Come up with the idea. Let's say you're looking for funds to professionally publish a local cookbook.
2. Choose the crowdfunding platform on which you're going to raise the money. (Some platforms don't allow certain types of fund-raising and/or fundraisers. We'll look more closely at this later.)

3. Write up your idea along with what the end result will be, how much money you're asking for, the risks to the contributors, the end date for your fund-raising effort, and (depending on the platform) the reward(s) for the contributors. Rewards are traditionally based on the amount a funder contributes. For this example, you could offer a PDF of the book for a $10 contribution, a paperback for $25, a hardcover for $50, and a hardcover autographed by all the authors for $250.
4. Promote your idea. You can do this through social media, your library's website, or print flyers—any way that will get the word out to your community. In every case, you should link back to the page for your project.
5. Throughout the length of your project, you should provide updates via the funding platform, keeping contributors and possible contributors up to date on your efforts.
6. When the end date arrives, collect your funds (minus the platform's fees) and implement your idea. On some platforms, if you don't achieve your funding goal, you don't get any of the money. On others, you get whatever amount was contributed. (Again, we'll look at this later.)

PROS AND CONS

The pros and cons of crowdfunding can be approached from two perspectives: those looking to receive the funds and those doing the funding.

The Fundraisers

For those looking to raise funds, crowdfunding platforms can provide a great way to advertise your project on a much wider scale. For example, Michael has contributed to library projects for libraries across the country. If those libraries had just advertised locally, they would not have had me as a contributor. The downside is that this can be a lot of work and, depending on the platform you choose, it may all be for naught. Remember, some platforms are all or nothing, while others allow you to collect the funds even if you don't make your goal.

For many municipal public libraries (those that are not self-funding districts), there is one piece of advice that applies here as well as to many other forms of fund-raising. You should seriously consider having your library friends group or foundation run your campaign. This way you can be sure the funds are available only to the library and are not part of your municipality's general fund. However, having a nonprofit organization run the campaign can have an impact on which platform you can use, so be sure to familiarize yourself with all of the rules before deciding on a platform.

The Funders

From the funder's perspective, you will get a great feeling knowing that you directly helped a person or organization achieve a goal, and you'll probably get some sort of reward for doing so. As a contributor, Michael has received a number of books and movies either earlier than the general commercial release or as part of a limited-edition run that was only available to contributors. The downside is that whenever you contribute, you are taking a chance on whether the item you're funding will actually appear. If you read the fine print, in most cases, the platform will not make a guarantee that the funds will be used as intended. Although so far we have received just about everything we've funded, a few projects have gone under and not delivered. In those cases, the fundees are not generally required to refund any money that they've collected. Jennifer's experience with this involved funding a maker-friendly, do-it-yourself (DIY) router setup. Though the goal was exceeded, the inventor had a personal crisis and never delivered on either the rewards or the final product.

CROWDFUNDING PLATFORMS

There are dozens of crowdfunding platforms available and more are being developed. Below we briefly introduce you to three of the larger and more popular ones.

Kickstarter (http://www.kickstarter.com)

Kickstarter (figure 4.1) is the oldest and most well known of the crowdfunding platforms. Everything, from art books to albums to feature films, has been funded here. On Kickstarter, if you don't achieve your funding goal, you don't get any of the money, and rewards for contributors are the norm, based on the amount contributed. Also, "Kickstarter does not allow projects to fundraise for charity or offer financial incentives."[2] Because of this, I have heard of libraries having their projects declined by Kickstarter.

Indiegogo (https://www.indiegogo.com/)

Indiegogo (figure 4.2) is the next largest of the platforms and seems to be a bit more open than Kickstarter regarding who can create projects and the types of projects that can be created. For example, Kickstarter generally expects that "something that can be shared" would come out of a project, whereas on Indiegogo, you could ask for funds to take a trip by yourself. Due

Figure 4.1.   Kickstarter.

Figure 4.2. Indiegogo.

to this different perspective on what constitutes a valid project, it seems that Indiegogo is more library-friendly.

GoFundMe (http://www.gofundme.com/)

GoFundMe (figure 4.3) focuses more on crowdfunding for individuals and charitable organizations that are looking for a new way to do fund-raising. The platform has plans for "Personal Campaigns," "Charity Fundraising," and "All-or-Nothing" campaigns. Years ago when Michael collected money to fund his honeymoon, he used a travel agent as the donation point. If he were to do that again today, he'd probably use GoFundMe instead.

LIBRARY APPLICATIONS

We've already provided you with one example of how a library could use crowdfunding to fund publishing a local cookbook. Later in this chapter, we'll list several specific examples of projects that libraries, librarians, and library-related organizations have completed. For now, let us propose a few more ideas as to the sort of projects a library could create.

- The library would like to bring a famous nonlocal author into the library for an event. This will require paying the author for his or her time and travel expenses. Advance funders could receive a ticket to the event at a cheaper rate than those purchasing tickets at a later time. Large contributors could earn a meet and greet with the author as a reward.
- The library would like to use some available space to create a multimedia studio available to the public. Some remodeling would be necessary to create a studio-quality space, and video and audio equipment would need to be purchased. The library would set a minimum goal for renovations and basic equipment. Additional funds would first buy better equipment and then fund extras (e.g., a green screen or a DJ turntable).

For any project, the crowdfunding platform you choose depends on everything discussed in the pro/con section, as well as the possible audience for the campaign. Chances are your audience for the project will be limited to those people in your service area. Yes, if you publish a book or create a website with your funds, there may be many outside of your area interested in funding you in exchange for a copy, but if you're trying to fund an event, chances are someone in another state will have much less interest in making a contribution. So when deciding how much money you're trying to raise, be sure to keep your project's audience in mind.

Figure 4.3.   GoFundMe.

CROWDFUNDING EXAMPLES

Here are a few examples of libraries, librarians, and library-related groups
that have used crowdfunding.

Fayetteville Fab Lab (https://www.indiegogo.com/projects/ ffl-fab-lab), Fayetteville Free Library, Syracuse, NY— Raised $13,670 of $20,000

The Fayetteville Free Library is excited to offer a new public service—the FFL
Fab Lab. What exactly is a fab lab? According to Neil Gershenfeld, the Director
of MIT's Center for Bits and Atoms and author of *Fab: the Coming Revolution
on Your Desktop—From Personal Computers to Personal Fabrication*, a fab lab
is "a collection of commercially available machines and parts linked by software
and processes developed for making things (Gershenfeld, 12)." At the foundation of the FFL's Fab Lab will be a MakerBot Thing-o-Matic 3D printer, made
available to the library through a generous donation from Express Computer
Services. . . .

We are asking for $20,000. This money will go towards purchasing more
technology for the FFL Fab Lab (more MakerBot's, a CNC Router, Lazor Cutter,
and MAC Lab), ABS plastic for our MakerBot (to help keep this service FREE
for the public), as well as bring in experts to give lectures and share their experience. The FFL has already received first round approval for a NY State Library
Construction Grant for $250,000 to renovate the east wing of the library. We also
won an Innovation Award of $10,000 from the Contact Summit on October 20th.
This project is happening now and your support will not only ensure its success,
but help us spread the word to other libraries across the country.

LibraryBox 2.0 (https://www.kickstarter.com/projects/griffey/ librarybox-20), Jason Griffey, Charlotte, NC—Raised $33,119 of $3,000

LibraryBox is an anonymous fileserver based on cheap hardware that runs on
little power and serves files to any wifi-enabled device with a browser. It is a
fork of the Open Source project PirateBox, altered to be more comfortable to use
for libraries, educators, and anyone else that has a need to serve files in locations
that lack reliable, unfiltered connectivity with the Internet.

LibraryBox is currently in use around the world by libraries, teachers, mu-
seums and more, in more than 7 countries on 5 continents. The v1.5 release is
useful, but with work LibraryBox can be much better. Moving towards the 2.0
release, there is a host of ways that LibraryBox could be better, should be better,
and this Kickstarter is a step towards making the LibraryBox project even more
useful. (Figure 4.4)

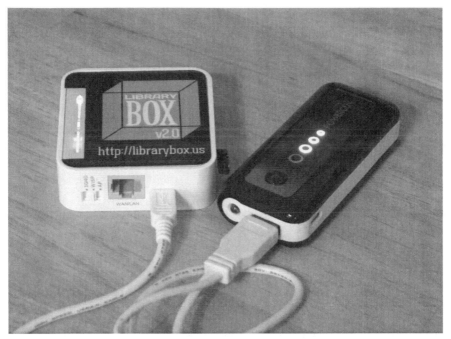

Figure 4.4. LibraryBox with associated cable and battery.

Bring the Hulk to the Northlake Public Library (https://www .indiegogo.com/projects/bring-the-hulk-to-the-northlake -public-library), Northlake Public Library, Northlake, IL —Raised $4,262 of $30,000

Libraries are constantly changing and evolving beyond just a place to do school work and use the internet. Today's libraries are celebrating creativity, entertainment and lifelong learning, and they are doing it with technology and popular materials including graphic novels. The problem is that many people still think of libraries in the old way. We want to smash that stuffy reputation with a 9 foot tall Incredible Hulk Statue.

Why The Hulk? Just as Dr. Bruce Banner transforms into the Hulk, we want our library community members to make their own personal transformations through books, programs, and awesome new equipment. This larger-than-life literary character will become a giant green beacon of light to highlight our graphic novel collection, our creation station . . . not to mention the library's sense of humor and whimsy. The project will show off the fun side of the library and get the community talking. The Hulk will force patrons to look at the library in a whole new way.

Library Ranger Badges (https://www.kickstarter.com/projects/billba/library-ranger-badges), Bill Barnes, Seattle, WA—Raised $33,298 of $7,000

A Library Ranger is anyone who loves libraries and helps support their mission, from librarians, pages, and clerks to teachers, students, and patrons. And now there's a fun way to celebrate the diverse skills that these good people exhibit on a daily basis: high-quality embroidered badges, designed by Bill & Gene, the Unshelved guys.

Wearing a Library Ranger badge tells the world that you are dedicated to executing your responsibilities, that you have completed your training with honors, that you performed service above and beyond the call of duty, or that you somehow managed to endure a truly epic level of nonsense. They are perfect for dazzling your friends, impressing your coworkers, or starting a conversation at a library conference. Give them to your employees, board members, supporters, volunteers, students, or yourself! (Figure 4.5)

Bring *Reading Rainbow* Back for Every Child, Everywhere! (https://www.kickstarter.com/projects/readingrainbow/bring-reading-rainbow-back-for-every-child-everywh), LeVar Burton and *Reading Rainbow*, Los Angeles, CA—Raised $5,408,916 of $1,000,000

Reading Rainbow's digital collection already contains hundreds of books and video field trips . . . but with your help, we'll be able to make the *Reading*

Figure 4.5.   Library Ranger badges.

Rainbow library available on more of the devices modern kids use to consume content. Now that we've met our initial goal of $1,000,000, we will be able to launch a new version of *Reading Rainbow* on the single most-used digital platform: the web. And now that we've reached our stretch goal of $5,000,000, we'll also be able to bring the service to mobile phones, Android, game consoles like XBOX and PlayStation, and set-top boxes like AppleTV and ROKU.

Additional Crowdfunding Projects

Neither of us have created a crowdfunding project of our own as of yet. However, we both have personally participated in several campaigns as funders, and these experiences informed this chapter. Here is just a sample of some of the projects we've participated in:

- Pebble smartwatch (https://www.kickstarter.com/projects/597507018/pebble-e-paper-watch-for-iphone-and-android; figure 4.6)
- Sidekick—Pebble Dock (https://www.kickstarter.com/projects/993722198/sidekick-pebble-dock; figure 4.6)
- C Is for Cthulhu: The Lovecraft Alphabet Board Book (https://www.kickstarter.com/projects/799956376/c-is-for-cthulhu-the-lovecraft-alphabet-board-book)

Figure 4.6. A Pebble smartwatch on the Sidekick dock.

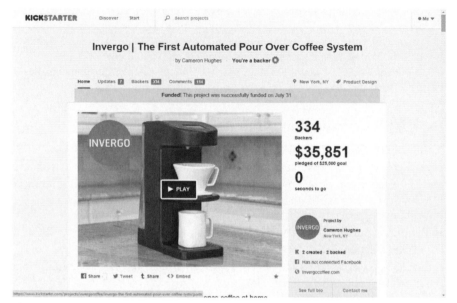

Figure 4.7.   Invergo.

- The H. P. Lovecraft Bronze Bust Project (https://www.kickstarter.com/projects/poebronzebust/the-hp-lovecraft-bronze-bust-project)
- We're Putting a TARDIS into Orbit—Really! (https://www.kickstarter.com/projects/573935592/were-putting-a-tardis-into-orbit-really)
- Invergo—the First Automated Pour-Over Coffee System (https://www.kickstarter.com/projects/invergocoffee/invergo-the-first-automated-pour-over-coffee-syste; figure 4.7)
- Brattle Theater: Digital Project and HVAC Renovation (https://www.kickstarter.com/projects/brattle/brattle-theatre-digital-projection-and-hvac-renova)
- *Emperor Norton's Stationary Marching Band: New Album* (http://www.pledgemusic.com/projects/ensmb?utm_campaign=project8899; figure 4.8). A good example of a change in the campaign as a result of a lower-than-expected response from funders. The band was originally raising money for a West Coast tour, and when that didn't reach a key campaign milestone, the band switched to raising money for a new album instead (which more local people really wanted, anyway). With this new focus, the band achieved its goal, and the album was released May 2015.
- 1732 Meats Processing Facilities Expansion (https://www.indiegogo.com/projects/1732-meats-expansion). An existing small meat-curing business wanted to expand its facilities to start mail orders and to reach beyond local farmer's markets. The campaign raised half of the requested funds.

Figure 4.8. *Emperor Norton's Stationary Marching Band: New Album.*

In the end, crowdfunding has a lot of possibilities, whether you have an idea that you'd like to get funded or would like to help fund. In these days of ever-tightening budgets, it behooves libraries to at least start to think about using crowdfunding as a way to support the services and programs that their communities are asking for.

NOTES

1. "Crowdfunding," *Wikipedia*, accessed February 26, 2015, http://en.wikipedia .org/w/index.php?title=Crowdfunding&oldid=619157364.

2. Kickstarter, "Kickstarter 101," Kickstarter Basics, accessed February 26, 2015, https://www.kickstarter.com/help/faq/kickstarter%20basics.

Chapter Five

Wearables

WHAT ARE WEARABLES?

The concept of wearable devices or wearable computing has been around for decades. In fact, researcher Steve Mann has been developing and documenting his own personal evolution of wearable computers since the mid-1980s.[1] However, these days the concept of wearable technology is becoming blurred as technology gets smaller and lighter. Even so, there is already starting to be some push-back on the term itself. Famed designer Syd Mead (*Blade Runner*, *Aliens*, *Tron*) has this to say:

Any consumer technology conversion is directed at consumer acceptance. Sometimes this works splendidly; sometimes all the guesses are wrong. Wearable technology is a term that is mindlessly inclusive. I mean, a special gym shoe with built-in pedometer and duration memory functions is "wearable technology." Wrist devices that monitor heartbeat, general blood consistency, etc., are "wearable technology," as are sweat-absorption clothing, electrically charged gloves, and other cold weather gear, and certainly visual augmentation devices.

I've been rendering many of these "new" ideas for decades. I illustrated both a fashion helmet in the '60s that combined a read-out screen for the wearer, a video pickup, and other functions that enabled the wearer to be reminded, guided, and allowed to upload.

I don't think the recent introductions into this technologically enabled consumer are either good or bad. The consumer acceptance will determine, as always, whether they persist or have to wait for a broader consensus. Google Glass, for instance, has acquired a geeky distinction of its own, becoming, in some social environments a disturbing intrusion into intra-personal ambiance. The more discreet devices, like the new Apple Watch and similar wrist keyboards will serve their purpose, though their usefulness doesn't go far beyond satisfying the early adopters' penchant for showing off how very, very clever they are.[2]

So to begin, let's describe what we're referring to as "wearable technology." For the purposes of this chapter, we're focusing on individual devices that will easily track personal data or interact with other devices such as a smartphone, or both.

Since most wearables are designed to track personal data about the wearer, let us briefly define the idea of the quantified self (QS). Wearable devices can tell us where we've been, how many steps we've taken, what our heart rate is, and more. QS is the idea that more and more of ourselves can be measured, quantified, stored, and tracked and that the accumulated data can be used to generate "self-knowledge through numbers." While we don't want to focus specifically on QS in this chapter (as that could easily be a whole book itself), several of the technologies we'll be presenting directly connect to that concept. For those readers interested in digging deeper into the idea of QS, read about it at the Quantified Self website (http://quantifiedself.com/).

PROS AND CONS

The many advantages of wearable technology may seem simple on the surface but in many cases boil down to the concept of convenience. For example, many people say that one of the biggest advantages to wearing a smartwatch that connects to your phone is that when certain things happen on your phone, you don't need to fish it out of your pocket to access the relevant information. Many other sarcastically counter that getting your phone out of your pocket is "so hard!" But let's look at it another way.

Michael has a Pebble smartwatch (described later in this chapter). When he receives a text message from a service he's trying to log in to that supports two-factor authentication (see chapter 7 for more details), instead of finding his phone, turning on the screen, reading a multidigit code, and typing it into his web browser, he can just lift his wrist, read the code, and type away. Another benefit is that his watch vibrates whenever he gets too far away from his phone (due to the fact that the Bluetooth connection has been broken) and therefore makes it much harder for him to accidentally leave his phone somewhere. These conveniences do come at a price, but whether it's worth the money is, as ever, left for each user to decide.

Of the downsides to wearable technology, the one that looms largest is privacy, especially when it comes to devices that work as trackers and information loggers. For example, if you wear an activity tracker such as a Fitbit, you can choose to make certain information, such as your step count, sleep patterns, and weight, public. While such services generally make this information private by default, even if you don't choose to make the information public you are still sharing this information with a company that could, in theory, share that information with others without your knowledge.[3] So while many people are fine with making such information "publically" available, others wish to keep it within a small group of friends and family, just to themselves, or prefer not to wear devices with any sort of online component. Each user must make a decision as to how comfortable he or she is with sharing or even collecting such data in the first place. Moreover, so far there's been at least one court case that included Fitbit data as evidence.[4] Granted that could work for you, but it also has the possibility to work against you depending on which side wants to use the data.

HARDWARE

Activity Trackers[5]

Fitbit (https://www.fitbit.com/)

The Fitbit (figure 5.1) was one of the earliest wearable activity trackers, and it is still one of the most popular. Available in several formats from clips to wristbands, at its most basic the Fitbit is a pedometer that will count your steps and upload the counts to your online account. Newer versions will also track your vertical ascent and count the stairs you have climbed in a day and/

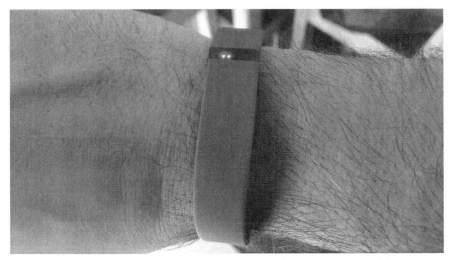

Figure 5.1. Fitbit Flex.

or track the quality of your sleep. Once the information is uploaded to your account, either via desktop/laptop computer or via a mobile app, you can keep your information private or share it with friends and have fun competing with them for the highest number of steps in a day. The Fitbit costs approximately $100.

Withings Pulse Ox (http://www.withings.com/us/withings-pulse.html)

The Withings Pulse Ox is a wristband device that tracks data points similar to those of the Fitbit, including steps, elevation, and sleep. However, this device is designed for the more active user: you can also put it in a jogging/running mode to display duration and distance statistics. Additionally, it tracks both your heart rate and blood oxygenation level. As with the Fitbit, data is logged to an online account via a mobile app and has gamification features such as earned badges. $199.95.

Nike+ Fuelband SE (http://www.nike.com/us/en_us/c/nikeplus-fuelband)

Also a wristband product, the Nike+ Fuelband is designed for the fitness enthusiast, with built-in extensive motivation features including the concept of NikeFuel, a "a single, universal way to measure all kinds of activities." While this band tracks similar data points to our two previous examples, it is designed to constantly sync with its partner mobile app for instantaneous and up-to-the-second information. The online account stores and presents your data either socially or privately and allows you to set challenges and goals for yourself and with friends. $99.

Life-Loggers

Narrative Clip (http://getnarrative.com/)

The Narrative Clip is a wearable 5MP camera that takes a photo every thirty seconds. You can also manually instruct it to take a photo by double-tapping it. To turn it off, just take it off and set it facedown.

> The Narrative Clip only weighs 20 grams (0.7 oz) and measures 36x36x9 mm (1.42x1.42x0.35 inches). With a storage capacity of 6000 pictures and battery life for 2 days of use, you can be sure to never miss a moment! Just plug it in to your computer to transfer all your images and recharge the batteries.[6]

If you check into the history of the Narrative Clip, you'll discover that it originally started out as the "Memoto" on Kickstarter (https://www.kick starter.com/projects/martinkallstrom/memoto-lifelogging-camera). This is an example of how one emerging technology (crowdfunding) can be used to develop another (wearables). $299.

Autographer (http://www.autographer.com/)

Autographer is a new type of camera which has been custom built to enable spontaneous, hands-free image capture. Its world-leading technology includes a custom 136° eye view lens, an ultra-small GPS unit and 5 in-built sensors. Autographer's five sensors (ambient light, accelerometer, magnetometer, PIR (passive infrared), and temperature) record a range of data which helps the camera decide when to take a photo. The readings are saved as metadata against each image which can be used as filters within your collection. These sensors are fused by a sophisticated algorithm to tell the camera exactly the right moments to take photos. ($399)[7]

Smart Watches

Pebble (https://getpebble.com/)

The Pebble smartwatch (figure 5.2) is the first generation of today's smartwatches and is still a popular choice for many. Originally created as a Kickstarter project (https://www.kickstarter.com/projects/597507018/pebble-e-paper-watch-for-iphone-and-android), the Pebble is cross-platform (pairing with both iOS and Android devices via Bluetooth), with an e-ink display that gives it a battery life of nearly a full week. Primarily designed to receive and

Figure 5.2. Pebble smartwatch.

display notifications from your phone, it also comes with an app store that allows users to add additional functionality, including displaying weather data, workout tracking, and checking in to locations via social networks. Currently the Pebble comes in an original and a steel version, made of plastic and metal accordingly. $99 and $199.

Samsung Gear 2 (http://www.samsung.com/us/mobile/wearable-tech/ SM-R3800MOAXAR)

Samsung's latest entry into the smartwatch field is based on the Android operating system. It features a 2-megapixel camera, 1.63-inch Super AMO-LED® (active-matrix organic light-emitting diode) display, stand-alone music player, and infrared blaster. It also allows users to respond to notifications via voice command. Its largest limitation is that it will only pair with select Samsung Galaxy phones. $299.

Motorola 360 (https://moto360.motorola.com/)

The Motorola 360 is the first smartwatch to fit into a new category of "Android Wear" devices. In this case, the watch is not dependent on a certain vendor's phones for pairing, though paired Android phones must have a current version of Android (4.3 or higher) in order to work. Notifications are based on the Google Now card system that is a feature on many Android phones. This watch features a color LCD screen, wireless charging, and battery life of one day. Apps that provide additional functionality are also available. $249.

Apple Watch (http://www.apple.com/watch/)

As of early 2015, Apple's first smartwatch has been announced and will be released in April 2015. It will be an iOS-based device and will pair with iPhones. There are various models, priced between $349 and $599.

Augmented and Virtual Reality

Google Glass (https://www.google.com/glass/)

Google Glass (figure 5.3) is actually two different kinds of wearable device in one. First, it's a smartwatch that you wear on your face—it provides notifications from a connected smartphone. Second, Glass is an information appliance in its own right, which allows you to communicate with a connected smartphone, request information, and have that information overlaid on the real world (e.g., augmented reality). Originally introduced in 2013 and available

Figure 5.3. Beth McCracken of Hastings Public Library (NE) wearing Google Glass. Copyright Mikel Philippi.

Google Glass

On January 15, 2015, Google cancelled the Glass Explorer program. In an e-mail sent to participants, Google stated:

> It's been an exciting ride. Since we first met, interest in wearables has exploded and today it's one of the most exciting areas in technology. We asked you to be pioneers, and you took Glass further than we ever expected. We've learned a ton, we've "graduated" from Google[x] labs, and now we're hard at work and you'll see future versions of Glass when they're ready. Since we're focusing all our efforts on the future, we'll be closing the Explorer Program on January 19. We realize you might have questions about what this means for you. New feature development on the Explorer Edition will stop while we work on the next version of Glass, but you can still call or email us anytime with questions, thoughts or feedback.

While this means that Google Glass is no longer available for purchase, it does indicate that the technology will continue on in another form. Sudden and unexpected change is an issue that libraries must deal with when it comes to cutting-edge technologies, a topic we discuss further in chapter 8.

as invitation only, Google Glass is now available to the general public, though due to its hefty price tag the product is still mainly targeted at developers and very early technology adopters.

Google Glass has a built-in 5MP camera that can take 720p video and broadcast live via YouTube. Audio is supplied via a Bone Conduction Transducer, and Glass's computer has 12MB of memory. The battery is designed to last about a day, but as with most batteries, this may be less depending on usage. $1,500.

Oculus Rift (http://www.oculus.com/rift/)

Though not the same type of "wearable" as Google Glass—you're not really meant to walk around while wearing it—the Oculus Rift is the latest in a long line of head-mounted virtual reality headsets designed for a fully immersive 3-D experience. Weighing in at just under one pound, the screen features a high-definition 720p resolution and full 360° head tracking. While neither of us have had a chance to physically test one of these devices, all reports say they are as impressive as they claim and are set to revolutionize virtual reality as we know it. This is yet another product that started its life as a Kickstarter project (https://www.kickstarter.com/projects/1523379957/oculus-rift-step-into-the-game). $350. (The consumer version was available for preorder at time of publication.)

PLATFORMS

All of the hardware that we have talked about in this chapter thus far have their own platforms. Fitbit data is uploaded to the Fitbit website, while Nike+ Fuelband data is uploaded to the Nike site. There are also several platforms available that allow you to collect and store data from multiple sources. Here are just two of them, both related to health data.

Daytum (http://daytum.com)

Whether you would like to tally an afternoon or a year, Daytum can help you collect and communicate the most important statistics in your life. From an up-to-the-moment personal dashboard, to a tabulation of an event, a home for sports scores, or as a corporate tool, the uses for Daytum may be limitless.

Daytum is free to use for as long as you like, but we also offer a Daytum Plus account for $4/month that offers additional features including the ability to collect and present more data, create pages and apply privacy settings to your account.[8]

Figure 5.4. Daytum.

While Daytum does have an iOS app, the app is for viewing and entering (figure 5.4). At this time, the service does not seem to have a way to automatically import data from other services or hardware.

Microsoft HealthVault (https://www.healthvault.com/)

Microsoft HealthVault (figure 5.5) is designed to "keep all of your health records in one place that's organized and available to you online."[9] Information that you can enter and store here include "medications, allergies, health history, fitness, blood pressure, lab results, conditions and illnesses, x-rays, scans, and many more kinds of health and wellness data."[10] Unlike Daytum,

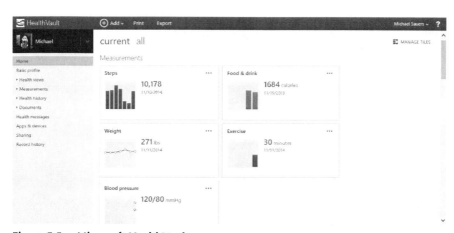

Figure 5.5. Microsoft HealthVault.

HealthVault has the ability to import a range of data from more than 130 other services, including CVS Pharmacy, the American Diabetes Association, and New York Presbyterian Hospital, and more than 220 devices, including the FitBit, blood pressure monitors, and blood glucose monitors.

Microsoft HealthVault accounts are free and have a full range of built-in privacy controls.

LIBRARY APPLICATIONS

As previously mentioned, Michael completely appreciates the two-factor authentication notifications he receives on his smartwatch. But what other notifications might a librarian appreciate receiving? Using a combination of technologies, the sky is practically the limit. If you can get the notification on a computer or a phone, there's probably a way to get it onto your smartwatch. How about being notified whenever a new chat reference session is started? This way you don't need to sit at a desk waiting for them to appear. You receive the notification on your watch and off to the desk you go. Depending on the features of the watch, maybe you can send a quick reply thanking the user for submitting a question and stating that you'll be available to help him or her momentarily.

Take this up a step to Google Glass and not only can you receive the notification, but if the question is coming through Google Hangouts, you can immediately start chatting with the patron and even show him or her exactly what you're doing and what you're looking at in order to help answer the question.

When it comes to the quantified self (QS) and wearables such as the Fitbit, library uses are a little less obvious. That said, if you combine the Google Glass reference question with QS data tracking, you could get useful data for library services. You can log the question and the time you start, record all the resources you use, track the number of steps you need to take throughout the building in order to answer the question. This data would be incredibly useful to libraries for staffing, planning, and requesting additional resources and staff.

Also, remember that it doesn't all have to be about the patrons. One of our examples at the end of this chapter is about a wellness program in the library workplace where the data collected was used to encourage colleagues to be more active and to earn prizes. In this case, it's more about making a pleasant workplace and happier, healthier employees. And happier employees can better serve the library's patrons.

Even though we're not even close to everyone wearing a computer at all times, the age of wearable technology is here and waiting for people with novel ideas about how to use it.

LIBRARY EXAMPLES

Oculus Rift Virtual Reality Headset, Arapahoe Library District, CO (http://arapahoelibraries.org/oculus-rift-demo-library), by Ginger Mattson, Manager of Strategic Marketing and Communications, Arapahoe Library District

The Arapahoe Library District (ALD), which serves more than 250,000 patrons in Colorado, purchased its first Oculus Rift in early 2014 as part of an effort to put difficult-to-access technology into the hands of patrons. Oculus Rift is a virtual reality headset that transports the wearer into a virtual 3-D world. The purchase of the Oculus Rift accompanied other difficult-to-access technology resources, such as Google Glass, 3-D printers, and more. Because the Oculus Rift is such an exciting and surprising experience, it has become a part of community outreach and marketing efforts as well. Picture a group of professional lawyers screaming like teenagers while riding a virtual roller coaster in the office conference room and you start to get the idea of the power of the Oculus Rift as an outreach tool.

Today, Arapahoe Library District owns eight pairs of the beta-technology headsets, which are featured as part of the library's "Show and Tech" technology road show. As a way to show nonlibrary users how libraries are changing, ALD takes these conversation-starting technologies on the road. Librarians, technology specialists, and marketing staff visit offices, set up at community events, and speak to professional organizations, computer clubs, and senior groups. While participants are busy trying out the technologies, library staff have the opportunity to introduce other library-related technologies and e-resources, such as downloadable e-books, audiobooks, music, and movies. The tech road shows are received with enthusiasm and a resounding, "I had no idea that libraries did that!"

Movband, Cleveland Public Library, Cleveland, OH (http://movable.com/our-impact/cleveland-public-library-circles-the-globe/), by Ronelle Miller-Hood, Payroll and Benefits Supervisor, Cleveland Public Library

Cleveland Public Library's (CPL) wellness committee, CPL FIT (Feeling Incredible Together) wanted to come up with a way that was fun, exciting, and motivating to get our employees moving. One of the issues uncovered on our very first health screening was our employees had high BMIs. We were pretty sure if we could just get our folks moving, BMIs would start to fall. So at one of our staff development days where we had all of our employees in one room we handed each of our employees a Movband (Moveable) and kicked off CPL's Race around the World.

CPL launched a Race around the World event where we broke our seven hundred employees into sixty teams by department/branch. The race started in June and ended in December of 2012. The teams used their Movbands to track their movement/miles and they entered their miles into a data base. We issued weekly updates on team standings and handed out colored markers for employees Movbands for milestone markers (1,000, 2,500, 5,000, 7,500 and 10,000 miles). The teams had a planned route and kept track of what country they were in by the number of miles they collectively walked. It was a fun competition among the departments/branches. We sent out weekly updates saying which teams where in the lead and which ones were catching up. Employees often looked at other employees' Movbands to see how many color markers they had and would often tease that they had more. Although we offered prizes for the three lead teams, which wound up being a healthy lunch and smoothie bar for the winning teams, I think the motivation wasn't the prize but the fact that they didn't want other departments/branches to win.

When all was said and done, our 700 employees visited over 44 countries and logged over 1/2 a million miles (509,691 miles to be exact).

I'm not sure if we can contribute these numbers all to Race around the World, but on our aggregate review with our wellness provider these were our results:

- Our population experienced a decrease in the percentage of participants who report obesity
- There was an increase in the desirable BMI category among the population
- Cleveland Public Library lost 1,751 pounds since last screening event
- 184 participants lost weight
- 60 participants lost 10 pounds
- 18 participants lost at least 20 pounds

Awesome results and a great way to begin our journey of getting healthier!

Our Race around the World challenge was two years ago now and our staff still wears their Movbands and still talks of the seven-month challenge. Our goal now is to come up with another challenge that can top Race around the World!

Google Glass, Hastings Public Library, Hastings, NE, by Jake Rundle, Collections Librarian, Hastings Public Library

In December of 2013, the Hastings Public Library had an opportunity to purchase Google's Glass product. When we initially saw the invitation, we thought "this would be really, really cool to have, but we have no idea what to do with it." When it arrived two days later, we again thought, "This is really, really cool, but what are we going to do with it?" Thankfully, after playing around with it for a few days, the possibilities opened up to us and we finally had some ideas with what we could be doing with this kind of tech.

First, we made it a goal to put Glass on the face of every middle school kid in the county. We picked middle school because (1) we have an excellent relationship with most of the middle school librarians and (2) middle school librarians convinced us that getting this kind of technology into the hands of middle school students would supply us with a more captive audience. Over the course of five months, we put Glass on the faces of over six hundred students in the county, as well as their teachers, coaches, and classroom aides. We've had students come to the library specifically to play with Glass, and we've had numerous requests to come back to the middle schools for more demonstrations.

Our other use of Glass is a little more mundane. The staff at the library were always forgetting to get pictures of programs happening at the library. Glass was a great way to wear a camera that was "always on" and also out of your hands. This also allowed frontline staff to familiarize themselves with technology that they wouldn't otherwise be using in their daily activities. Staff were hesitant to try something that was so expensive, but showing them how to use the camera feature helped them ease into the technology.

NOTES

1. "Steve Mann," *Wikipedia*, accessed September 27, 2014, http://en.wikipedia.org/w/index.php?title=Steve_Mann&oldid=626262182.

2. Mark Wilson, "The Problem with Wearable Technology, according to 'Blade Runner' Designer Syd Mead," *Wearables Week* (blog), October 2010, http://www.fastcodesign.com/3036532/wearables-week/the-problem-with-wearable-technology-according-to-blade-runner-designer-syd-m#5.

3. In every case we've checked, the companies in question all have had privacy policies in place. However, that isn't necessarily a guarantee that those policies can't or won't change in the future.

4. Parmy Olsen, "Fitbit Data Now Being Used in the Courtroom," *Forbes*, November 16, 2014, http://www.forbes.com/sites/parmyolson/2014/11/16/fitbit-data-court-room-personal-injury-claim/.

5. There are several different ways that you can organize wearables in to categories. We've decided to do it more by function, while others do it by the item's location on the body. For a longer list of "wrist wearables," check out Ernesto Ramirez, "Wrist Wearables: How Many Are There?" Quantified Self, accessed February 26, 2015, http://quantifiedself.com/2014/09/wrist-wearables-now/.

6. "The Narrative Clip," Narrative, accessed February 26, 2015, http://get narrative.com/narrative-clip-1.

7. Autographer, "Photography Reinvented," Autographer Accessories, accessed February 26, 2015, http://www.autographer.com/accessories#accessories.

8. "Features," Daytum, accessed February 26, 2015, http://daytum.com/about/features.

9. Microsoft, "Overview," HealthVault, accessed February 26, 2015, https://www.healthvault.com/us/en/overview.

10. Microsoft, "Overview."

Chapter Six

The Internet of Things

WHAT IS THE INTERNET OF THINGS?

Over the past decade, computers have become a part of our daily lives, and we may not even recognize how interconnected their uses are. OnStar services in cars, remote toll transponders like E-ZPass, transponders connecting to your credit card at the gas pump, remote wireless photo frames, Wi-Fi-enabled digital cameras—all are networked physical devices communicating over the Internet to improve your life. In the library world, RFID chips in materials and even QR codes in the library stacks that connect physical collections directly to online resources have been part of the early Internet of Things.

The Internet of Things is precisely this: everyday objects that are connected to the Internet and to each other through tiny embedded computers. More important, most of these smart devices can also sense what is happening around them and communicate that information both to other things and back to a central application, system, or platform. As Internet connectivity via Wi-Fi or cellular networks becomes ubiquitous, it is possible for any object at home, in schools, at work, on the road, or anywhere else to be a part of this vast network of devices and information.

Today an app on a smartphone can receive reports from sensors and smart devices in a home and allow a user to

- unlock or lock a door;
- turn the HVAC and lights on or off or change the color of LED lights;
- get security alarm updates, including images from a webcam;
- play media on a mobile device at home, or operate a device at home remotely (for after-school kids or vacation security);

Figure 6.1. Using DIY devices and networks or vendor-controlled systems, you can monitor and control most of the basic functions of your home remotely.

- get information about water leaks or how efficient your fridge is today; and
- view a video feed from baby and pet monitors (figure 6.1).

In hospitals, patient monitoring devices can be reviewed remotely by doctors anywhere via a network connection, including the personal insulin pumps worn by people with diabetes. Trucks fitted with sensors can assist their drivers in keeping themselves and other vehicles safe on the roads and also report back on traffic conditions for use by other trucks in the fleet. High-end products can keep track of their own maintenance and transmit a need for updates or repairs back to the manufacturer or owner. Few of these connected things are intelligent on their own—it's only as part of a larger network of sensors and information that they become truly useful.

Now imagine the future. Chips in the products in your kitchen and sensors in the fridge and cabinets keep a running account of what you have in stock. You're in the grocery store on your way home and via a recipe app, you decide what you want to make for dinner. The cabinet monitor app on your phone takes the recipe information, checks what you have in stock, and produces a shopping list that you know is 100 percent accurate, and you don't end up with yet another box of couscous.

PROS AND CONS

With an ever-increasing network of smart devices, it's easy to remote control your life from your phone or tablet. Remote awareness and control can mean improved security, efficiency, and accountability in all areas of life. In addition, the data collected by all these sensors contribute to the growing field of Big Data, massive computations based on input from millions of sources to see larger patterns and make better predictions about behavior and the future.

However, the rapid growth of the Internet of Things has sparked many concerns around its implementation now and in the future. For users, the cost, longevity, and usefulness of these smart devices has to be proven worthwhile over time. Very few people will install a smart deadbolt if it costs significantly more than its "dumb" predecessor and constantly needs upgrades or replacement. More important, there has to be some utility to a smart device beyond the fact that it's connected to a network of other devices. In the case of our deadbolt, it's easy to see that being able to remotely lock a door you've left open by accident is worth its weight in gold, but other smart devices may not be so obviously useful.

Two other areas of real concern are security and interconnectivity. Recent upswings in large systems of personal information being hacked and sensitive details being stolen have increased concerns about network security both by consumers and professionals. We'll look more closely at security in the next chapter, but for the Internet of Things, it's even more worrisome: there have already been reports of hackers breaking into audio/video baby monitoring systems and causing a disturbance,[1] and as connected home security systems and controls become more popular, will we see increased personal property crime and damage?

As with most other major technological breakthroughs, the Internet of Things is causing rifts in the communications standards that different devices and networks use to talk to each other. Without diving too deeply, it's enough to know that the tech industry is already working to create widely accepted standards for the protocols that link devices and their controlling networks. The Internet of Things will not succeed in its goals of universal functionality and massive amounts of data if everything is speaking a different language.

INTERNET OF THINGS SERVICES AND PLATFORMS

Due to its nature, we can't cover even a strong sampling of the current and future services, devices, and platforms for the Internet of Things. This is truly emerging technology and is exploding in scope and complexity. Instead, we'll focus on late 2014 technologies that your patrons are most likely to encounter.

Home Automation and Security Systems

All of the following systems are comprehensive, home-wide security and remote-control systems that allow owners to monitor security, turn lights on or off, start and stop appliances and media players, open standard swinging doors and garage doors, and more, all from an app on a smartphone or a web interface (figure 6.2).

- Control4—http://www.control4.com/
- Skylink—http://www.skylinkhome.com/
- SmartThings—http://www.smartthings.com/

Traditional Products Made Smart

There are also individual products that have had smart technology added to them, allowing them to be connected to a home Internet of Things. These modular pieces of the network are a more likely first step into the connected home for people coming into the library to ask questions.

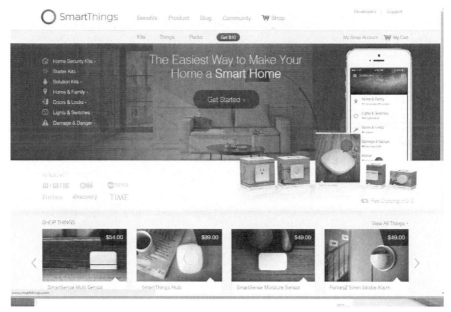

Figure 6.2. SmartThings allows anyone to create a network of connected home controls.

Most modern televisions, receivers, Blu-ray players, and game consoles are already connected to the Internet of Things via a cable or digital satellite connection. If not, media streaming devices such as Google's Chromecast (http://www.google.com/chrome/devices/chromecast/) and Nexus Player (http://www.google.com/nexus/player/), Roku (http://www.roku.com), and BiggiFi (http://biggifi.com) plug into the television and bring the Internet of Things to "dumber" devices (figure 6.3).

Baby monitors used to be restricted in range and information—sound traveled from the baby to you via a dedicated (and clunky) speaker that had to be placed within a certain distance from the crib. Now baby monitors include both video feeds and two-way sound, and they also can feed directly to a smartphone for remote monitoring. Even if there's a babysitter at home, parents can watch and sing to their little one at bedtime from wherever they are.

The Chui (http://www.getchui.com) is an intelligent doorbell that uses facial recognition to unlock the door and then enables smart devices in your home to turn on or change settings as you walk in.

Phillips lighting entered the smart device market with the Hue wireless light bulb. Why a light bulb? Rather than depend on a system or even a separate device to turn on or off a whole fixture, the Hue allows each bulb to be controlled remotely. A single lamp with multiple bulbs can be controlled light by light, changing the ambiance and the mood.

Figure 6.3. The Chromecast player, combined with the Chrome browser or a third-party system like Plex, lets any HDMI-compatible television become a connected device.

Similarly, the Kevo from Kwikset (http://www.kwikset.com/kevo/default .aspx)—a Bluetooth-enabled deadbolt—lets you use your smartphone as a key, or you can use the included fob if you don't have a smartphone. Beyond the personal convenience, the Kevo eKey can be sent directly to the smartphone of anyone you'd like to authorize to enter your home: a guest, relative, or contractor. Those eKeys can be suspended or deleted instantly, so there's no need to worry about getting your keys back from anyone.

Originally funded by a Kickstarter project, the Rocki (http://www.myrocki. com/) connects to any speaker in your home and allows you to stream music from your smartphone, controlled by the Rocki app. Have speakers in different rooms or attached to your computer? Just buy a few more $50 Rockis and have one per setup. Rocki takes the same input jack as a set of headphones, so you could carry around a few Rockis connected to your app and stream your music directly into your friend's headphones or any portable audio player or speakers.

In 2011, New York City's ConEdison introduced the coolNYC program (http://www.coolnycprogram.com). Each participant received a modlet (a smart wireless outlet) and a smart modlet thermostat, both of which could be controlled by an app on a smartphone. The hope was that the program would reduce unnecessary air conditioner use during the day, when most people are

Figure 6.4. coolNYC used smart outlets and smart thermostats to encourage residents of all income levels to use connected technologies in order to increase home electrical efficiency.

at work, by allowing them to remotely turn on the AC while they are on their way home or by programming in a set schedule for air conditioner use each day (figure 6.4).

Connected cars could be an entire chapter on their own, but the most important thing to know is that they are already smart and getting smarter all the time. From OnStar accident reporting to GPS, from rearview video feeds and sensors to Bluetooth-enabled radios, most modern cars have many of the basic elements for the Internet of Things. The car itself is becoming a Wi-Fi hub for additional devices, as seen in the Chevy lines of 4G/LTE-enabled vehicles.[2] Newer features include vehicle-to-vehicle communication for accident avoidance, auto-routing assists via GPS, cars reading e-mails and texts out loud, remote monitoring of systems (the new electric BMW i3 has an app that lets you check battery capacity during recharge), communication between car and traffic signaling (there is a current University of Michigan experiment testing this on real roads), driverless steering (Mercedes-Benz has the "Intelligent Drive" system for driverless steering in traffic under 60 kph), and much more. Even the current trend of car sharing "will be far easier when communication between vehicles and potential passengers is seamless and any car can be accessed and operated securely by any smartphone. Making journeys using several forms of transport, including a car, will be smoother if it is easier to find car-sharing locations or parking spaces close to connecting points for trains or buses."[3]

Do-It-Yourself Sensors and Controllers

Unsurprisingly, the DIY/maker movement has dived headfirst into the Internet of Things. Thousands of sensors, controllers, apps, and other tools allow anyone to fully customize his or her own connected world. Let's look at a few examples.

Nest Products (http://nest.com/) and Dropcam (http://dropcam.com/)

Nest, one of the early, well-known smart device companies, offers both an app-controlled thermostat and smoke/carbon monoxide sensor (figure 6.5). The Dropcam, also by Nest, is a simple wireless video monitor that connects with the Nest system and other smart home monitoring systems.

iSmartAlarm (http://www.ismartalarm.com/Home) and SmartThings (http://www.smartthings.com/)

The iSmartAlarm is a DIY app-controlled security system. SmartThings (mentioned previously) is another DIY system but includes home monitoring and remote-controlled devices as well as security tools.

Figure 6.5.   The Nest thermostat allows you to control the temperature remotely.

Bt.tn (http://bt.tn/)

Bt.tn is a single large button that can be programmed to turn lights on or off, open or lock doors, or simply send a text message or e-mail when pressed (figure 6.6). Suggested uses include an easy way for children to let their parents know that they're home safe from school or to remind older patients to take their (often numerous) medications.

Estimote Beacons and Stickers (http://estimote.com)

Estimote beacons and stickers allow you to add "contextual awareness" to any environment—say, a library—by using tiny computers that communicate wirelessly with nearby smartphones (figure 6.7). Each beacon or sticker can be programmed to connect to an Estimote app and have a specific response: suggest a route, offer additional information, submit analytic information, and more.

If This, Then That (http://ifttt.com)

If This, Then That (IFTTT) is a simple interface that you can use to create "if this happens, then do that" relationships between applications, devices, and many combinations of the two. Using the simple "if this, then that" formula,

Figure 6.6.   The bt.tn can be used as a controller for any smart device paired with a system like If This, Then That.

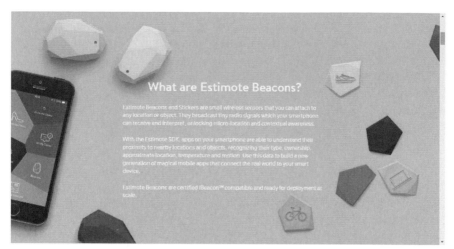

Figure 6.7. Estimote beacons and stickers apply to any surface.

you can create connections between smart devices and controllers ("if the
Bt.tn is pressed, then turn on this Hue light bulb") or between smart devices
and apps ("if my Fitbit logs steps, then send an update to a Google spread-
sheet every half hour").

ThinkEco Modlet (http://www.thinkecoinc.com/)

The modlet from ThinkEco is a wirelessly controllable outlet used in the
coolNYC program mentioned earlier (figure 6.8). Any appliance plugged into
the modlet (which is plugged into a standard wall outlet) can be upgraded to
a smart device. ThinkEco also offers a specific air conditioner kit that uses
the same technology to add programmable temperature control to any AC.

Sonos (http://www.sonos.com)

Sonos is a well-established wireless home theater system that integrates easily with your own music library as well as with streaming music services like
Spotify and Pandora and is controlled by an app on your phone.

Notion Sensor (http://notion.is/)

The Notion sensor, a funded Kickstarter project, is a low-cost home intel-
ligence system that is truly smart: each sensor includes an accelerometer (to
detect someone knocking on a door), temperature and water leak sensors,
proximity sensors, ambient light sensors ("Did I leave the lights on?" is finally answerable), and more (figure 6.9). The Notion may well be the next

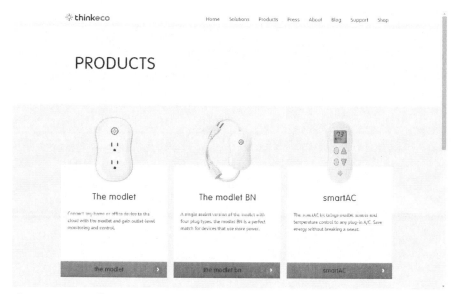

Figure 6.8. Modlet and SmartAC from ThinkEco.

big thing: the project's original Kickstarter goal was $50,000, and nearly $300,000 was pledged.

NFC Tags

There are also more gadget-generic ways to build your own Internet of Things. Near-field communication (NFC) "tags"—small programmable NFC-activated computer chips attached to stickers—can be placed nearly anywhere and interact with a smartphone to complete specific actions (like the Bt.tn and Estimote stickers above). Use IFTTT or another tool to create connections between the action of the NFC tag and an app on your smartphone.

Amazon Echo (http://www.amazon.com/oc/echo)

Finally, in late 2014, Amazon entered the Internet of Things with the Amazon Echo, a voice-activated device that connects to your Amazon account and allows you to play music, add items to your Amazon shopping cart, get information and answers from news sites and Wikipedia, set timers, and connect to your mobile devices to stream other audio sources such as Spotify or Pandora. Right now, Amazon Echo is more of a voice-activated shopping cart than a true controller, but if it's successful, Amazon might add a connection to IFTTT or another system for additional functionality.

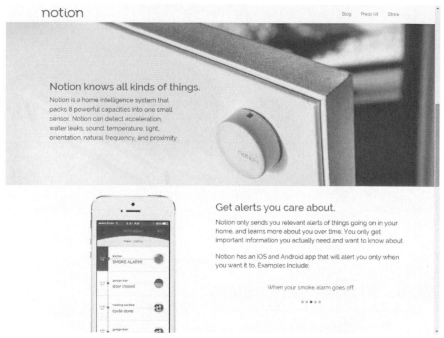

Figure 6.9. Using devices like the Notion, more tech-savvy users can create customized, DIY systems that don't rely on expensive companies.

LIBRARY EXAMPLES

The Internet of Things is still so new that there aren't any examples of its use in libraries yet. Right now, the most important things to know and understand about the Internet of Things is that it's coming and that many of our users either don't know that parts of their home are already connected to that network or they don't fully understand what that means or how to manage it.

Libraries are perfectly poised to help educate users on the technologies and ideas behind the Internet of Things, the importance of software and firmware upgrades and how those affect their security, and the ramifications of a fully connected life. We need to make sure our patrons are supported in their use of these technologies in the rest of the world.

That being said, the beginnings of the Internet of Things are expanding in libraries beyond automated materials sorting and retrieval and the fading presence of QR codes. Many libraries using RFID chips on their materials have moved to the next generation of self-checkout stations. Rather than needing to scan a library card and each item's barcode, RFID-enabled self-checkout can read the smart chip in a library card, check out an entire stack of materials at once, and automatically print a receipt. The kiosk-less checkout at the National Library Board of Singapore that we saw in chapter 3 allows borrowers to scan a barcode with an app and check items out on the fly. Eventually, a smart chip inside a library card or an app on a smartphone, combined with something like the Estimote beacon, will allow patrons to simply pick out their materials, pass through security gates, and check out as they walk out the door. We have been hearing about this in the retail world for years, but a true Internet of Things would make it a reality.

Perhaps the real future is a fully chipped library with automated item retrieval, allowing a user at home to check out a physical object from the library, have a robot arm pull it from the collapsible stacks, and drop it into the delivery system that will route it to a driverless bookmobile or individual remote drone, which then delivers the item to your door. Don't laugh—we are talking about the future, after all.

ADDITIONAL READINGS

For more information about the state of the Internet of Things in late 2014, we suggest these articles and whitepapers:

- The Pew Research Center's Internet and American Life Project report on the Internet of Things: http://www.pewinternet.org/2014/05/14/internet -of-things/
- Two excellent articles describing the Internet of Things from a business perspective: http://www.infoworld.com/article/2614273/it-management/ the-internet-of-things—coming-to-a-network-near-you.html and http:// www.networkworld.com/article/2164484/smb/what-is-the-internet-of -things-.html
- The online news magazine *Quartz* has a tag for the Internet of Things so readers can quickly locate articles: http://qz.com/on/internet-of-everything/
- In late summer 2014, researchers at IBM released a whitepaper on the current concerns surrounding the Internet of Things and offering some possible solutions: http://www-935.ibm.com/services/us/gbs/thought leadership/internetofthings/

NOTES

1. "Home, Hacked Home: The Perils of Connected Devices," in "Cyber-Security," special report, *Economist*, July 12, 2014, 14.

2. General Motors/Chevrolet, list of current features for 4G/LTE-enabled cars, accessed November 29, 2014, http://www.chevrolet.com/culture/article/4g-lte.html.

3. "The Connected Car: Smartphones on Wheels," in "Technology Quarterly: Q3 2014," *Economist*, September 6, 2014, 18.

Chapter Seven

Privacy and Security

WHY PRIVACY AND SECURITY?

We saved this chapter for second to last because all of the previous technologies we've presented will have an impact on and be impacted by privacy and security issues. Perhaps more important, privacy and security are moving targets. When talks were beginning with regard to the writing of this book, the revelations by Edward Snowden regarding the level of surveillance in the NSA had not yet come to light. While writing early drafts of this book, the Heartbleed SSL bug[1] was discovered, forcing many people to change every password on every online system they used; later drafts were accompanied by the Shellshock vulnerability[2] and an SQL flaw that affected Drupal users.[3] By the time you read this, we are almost certain that there will have been other major privacy and security news stories that we cannot predict.

What we hope to do in this chapter is to address some of the issues of privacy and security and point you at some of the technologies available to help anyone keep their data as private and as secure as possible, yet still allowing you to participate in the online world.

PROS AND CONS

We hope that the pros to both privacy and security are generally obvious to the reader. But to make sure we cover the bases, allow us to make a few salient points:

First, it is generally no one else's business what you are doing online unless you choose to share that information. This goes double for what patrons are doing in the library. It is a core part of our ethics as librarians—and state law in most cases—that the privacy of patron records is to be protected and only made available under a court order. However, a library can't share records that it doesn't have, and many libraries choose not to retain patron borrowing information after items are returned.

Second, when it comes to security, we believe that it is the responsibility of the library to assist patrons in learning how to secure themselves and their information and to provide as secure an environment as realistically possible when it comes to the public computers.

Third, it will be harder to address both of these issues for our patrons if we are not at least minimally versed in these issues ourselves. Both privacy and security affect librarians as much as they affect library patrons; the better you are able to help yourself, the better you'll be able to help your patrons.

But it is important to point out that there can be a downside to increased privacy and security: inconvenience. Using the tools that are available to make yourself more private and/or secure are inconvenient to some degree. Something as simple as a longer, more complex password will take longer to remember, longer to type in, and is easier to mistype. Some tools that increase your privacy will, by design, slow down your connection to the Internet. In both cases, frustration can easily ensue.

In the end, the balance between security and convenience must always be considered. However, in these times, with more and more information being stored online, we strongly encourage you to consider giving up at least some of the convenience you've become accustomed to. It may be frustrating at first, but you'll benefit in the long run.

PRIVACY AND SECURITY SOFTWARE

Privacy

There are several different ways you can protect your online privacy these days without too much hassle. The first two we'll discuss are free and can be applied easily in both a home and a library setting; the third will involve a medium level of cost (depending on the number of computers involved) and is less useful in the home than it is in a public-computing setting.

Your Browser's Private Browsing Mode

All of the current major Internet browsers (Internet Explorer,[4] Firefox,[5] Chrome,[6] and Safari[7]) support some sort of "private browsing." Though not the default state, each of these browsers can be put into a "private" mode, which prevents certain bits of information from being saved to the computer when the browser is closed.

Figure 7.1. Chrome's Incognito mode.

For example, here is what Chrome will do when you use its "Incognito" mode (figure 7.1):

- *Your browsing history isn't recorded.* The webpages you open and the files you download in Incognito mode aren't recorded in your browsing and download histories.
- *Your cookies are deleted.* All new cookies are deleted after you close all Incognito windows.
- *You can switch easily between Incognito and regular mode.* You can have both Incognito mode windows and regular windows open at the same time, and switch between the two.
- *Extensions are disabled.* Your extensions are automatically disabled in Incognito windows. This is because Google Chrome does not control how extensions handle your personal data. If you want an extension to show up in Incognito windows, select the extension's "Allow in Incognito" checkbox.[8]

The Tor Browser

The Tor browser (https://www.torproject.org/projects/torbrowser.html.en), a product of the Tor Project (https://www.torproject.org/) takes a slightly different approach when it comes to keeping your browsing private. In this case it "protects you by bouncing your communications around a distributed network of relays run by volunteers all around the world: it prevents somebody watching your Internet connection from learning what sites you visit,

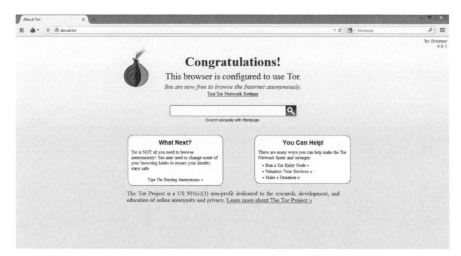

Figure 7.2.   The Tor browser.

it prevents the sites you visit from learning your physical location, and it lets you access sites which are blocked" (figure 7.2).[9]

By using the Tor browser, the site on the other end has no real idea where you are physically located, something that is generally trivial for sites to figure out. Additionally, the Tor browser comes with privacy-related plug-ins preinstalled, such as HTTPS Everywhere (https://www.eff.org/https-everywhere) and NoScript (https://addons.mozilla.org/en-US/firefox/addon/noscript/), two add-ons that we highly recommend you install even on a regular browser for added security. Based on the way the Tor browser is configured, it works similarly to a private browsing mode, by default and by design. Lastly, there are even whole websites or versions of websites that can only be accessed using the Tor network. For example, in the fall of 2014, Facebook started offering a Tor-only version of their site located at https://facebookcorewwwi.onion/, a URL that will only work once you're connected to the Tor network.

It is possible to run the Tor service at the computer and/or network level and force all traffic to be anonymized as it leaves the computer or network. However, this is a much more drastic action and isn't something that we recommend doing in a library setting.

The downside that we must mention here is that by running traffic through the Tor network, regardless of the connection method, your Internet will be slower; chances are that it will be noticeably slower. As we mentioned earlier in this chapter, you need to weigh the inconvenience of a slower connection against the enhanced privacy you'll gain.

Resetting Public Computers: Faronics Deep Freeze and
Centurion SmartShield

Anyone who has worked with public access computers in a library is probably aware of one or both of these programs already. Both Faronics Deep Freeze (http://www.faronics.com/products/deep-freeze/), and Centurion SmartShield (http://www.centuriontech.com/smartshield.aspx) have been around in one form or another for more than a decade and are commonly found in libraries. The central benefit to either program (or others of this type) is that when installed it prevents any changes to the computer from becoming permanent post-reboot. Basically, you can allow your patrons to do anything they'd like to the computer and, once you reboot it, the computer will return to exactly the same state as you left it when you locked it down.

As you may quickly figure out, there are both privacy and security implications with these programs, hence our placement of them here at the end of the privacy section, leading into the security section.

From a privacy standpoint, if a patron leaves sensitive information on the computer, it will be automatically removed upon reboot. The same will happen should someone leave their Google account logged in: Reboot and the login information is gone.

From a security perspective, these programs let your patrons do what they wish, including whatever maliciousness they may want to get up to (reformatting the hard drive, for example), and a reboot solves the problem. If a patron accidently downloads a virus, that is also cleaned up with a reboot.[10]

The downside to using reset software is twofold. First, these programs are not free. Pricing for both programs start at around $50 per computer, but site licensing and discounted purchasing is available if you look around. Second, the programs do add a layer of complexity to the computer when it comes to basic administration. Features differ, but you may need to "turn off" the software in order to run updates or make minor changes, and depending on the number of computers you have, this can add significant time to the process.

Security

Like it or not, the single greatest point of failure when it comes to staying secure online is your passwords. Please notice that we said passwords plural, not singular. You do have different passwords for different systems and services, right? If not, please consider this your first piece of advice in this area: *do not* reuse passwords. Then again, we're pretty sure you've heard this advice before, along with the rest of the common wisdom when it comes to choosing good passwords: the longer the better and the more types of characters (upper and lower case, numbers, and symbols) the better.

The problem inherent in this advice is that it means that great passwords are hard to remember. Sure, there are methods for creating pretty good passwords using things like phrases and character substitutions, but truly great passwords are as random and as long as possible. So what's available today that can help you achieve better online security? There are three types of software we'll be discussing: password managers, two-factor authentication, and virtual private networks (VPNs).

Password Managers

Password managers such as LastPass (https://lastpass.com/), 1Password (https://agilebits.com/onepassword), and Meldium (http://www.meldium.com) are software packages that have both off-line and online features to allow you to securely store and retrieve all of your passwords. All of these programs have similar functionality and features, but since we're users of LastPass, we'll focus on it in order to show you how software of this type works.

The key functionality of LastPass (figure 7.3) is its ability to store your login credentials, along with any other information you care to give it, securely in the cloud. Your information is stored using 256-bit AES encryption, meaning that without the single LastPass password you set on your account, even if someone was to capture the whole of the LastPass database, that person would only end up with an incomprehensible blob of meaningless text. So the first key is to sign up with LastPass; choose a single, good password; and then let it take over from there.

Figure 7.3. The LastPass interface in Chrome.

Once installed in your browser via a plug-in, you can use LastPass to create complex passwords when you sign up for new services and let LastPass handle logging in to those services when you return. (We recommend also changing all of your old, bad passwords to new ones using LastPass.)

So, for example, when Michael signs up for a new online service, he tells LastPass to generate a sixteen-character, completely random password and use that in order to create his account. He then instructs LastPass to remember that service's URL, his username, and his password. Later, when he returns to log in to that service, LastPass pops up and asks him for his LastPass password. He enters that, then LastPass passes the correct credentials to the site and he's logged in. At this point, Michael doesn't have any idea what any of his passwords actually are. All he needs to do is remember one.

Since all of this information is stored in the cloud, even if Michael is on a computer that he doesn't control and/or that doesn't have LastPass installed, he can log in to his LastPass account via a web browser and easily access his password database in order to copy and paste the necessary information.

It is important to note that this does somewhat slow down the process of logging into sites. More important, if you were to forget that one password, there's no way to retrieve it, so make sure it's something sufficiently complex yet still memorable.

There are some additional features available in most password managers, such as a security check to both report weak passwords in your account or check for systems with known breaches so you can change your password for those logins. All three programs are free, but LastPass does have a $12/year premium version that gives you access to a LastPass smartphone app, providing you with the same abilities on your phone as on your desktop.

Two-Factor Authentication

Passwords are considered single-factor authentication. In other words, there is only one point of authentication when you access an account, when you use a piece of information you know (your password). Two-factor authentication adds an additional step to a login process: something you know (your password) and something you have. But how can a website know what you have?

First, you need to find a service that supports two-factor authentication, since not all online services support it and the ones that do require you to turn it on or opt in. Let's use Twitter as our example, since it's one of the less-complex options.

If you log in to your Twitter account and go to *Settings, Security and privacy*, you'll find a section labeled "Login verification." To turn on two-factor authentication, select "Send login verification requests to [your cellphone number]." Once you've done that, every time you log in to Twitter from a

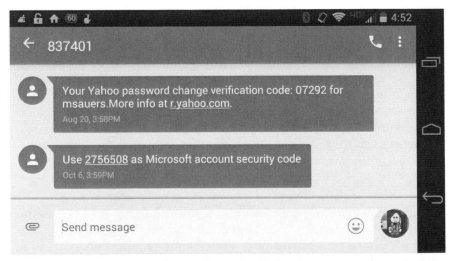

Figure 7.4.   Second-factor authentication codes displayed on a smart phone via SMS.

new computer, after you enter your username and password (something you know), a text message will be sent to your phone (something you have) containing a short numerical code (figures 7.4 and 7.5). You must then enter that code into Twitter before being granted access to your account.

Assuming you're the person trying to access your account from a new computer, this is generally a minor inconvenience. (Assuming you have your phone with you.) However, if it isn't you trying to access your account from

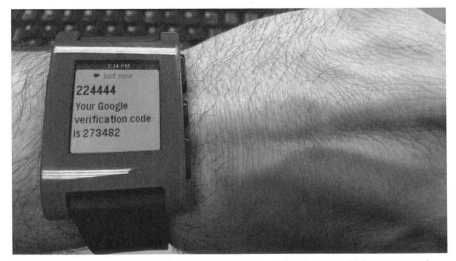

Figure 7.5.   Second-factor authentication notice displayed on a Pebble smartwatch.

the other side of the world, this is a great way to easily stop unauthorized access.

More and more online systems are implementing two-factor authentication every day. Sites like Google, Facebook, and PayPal are just a few of the larger sites using it. Some services have additional two-factor options beyond text messages, including hardware key fobs and dedicated second-factor apps. Be sure to check out the available options with each service, as one method might work better for you than another.

Virtual Private Networks

Simply put, a virtual private network (VPN) is a way to securely connect multiple computers to each other over the inherently insecure open Internet. There are generally two ways to accomplish this using a VPN. The first is to connect from one computer to another in which you control both ends of the connection. This ensures that any data you transfer between those two computers is secure and safe from eavesdropping. The second is to use an online service that can give you a secure connection through their network of computers. This method not only secures your traffic from eavesdropping but can easily mask where you are physically located for an added level of privacy. Let's take a look at TeamViewer and CyberGhost, which use the previously mentioned methods, respectively.

TeamViewer. TeamViewer (http://www.teamviewer.com/) is a free program for noncommercial use that, once installed on both ends, allows the user of one computer to create a secure connection to another computer (figure

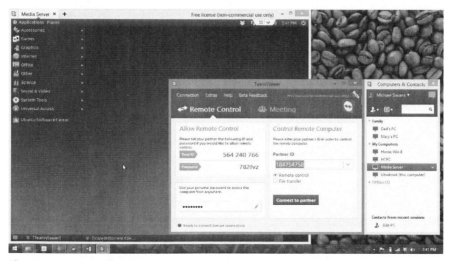

Figure 7.6. TeamViewer.

7.6). Once this connection is made, users can perform secure chat and file transfer along with viewing and control of the remote computer. Beyond the obvious technical support uses, TeamViewer can increase the security of connections using open Wi-Fi access points. For example, when connected to an open Wi-Fi signal, a user can run TeamViewer and remotely connect to their computer at home, then perform tasks such as web surfing over the secured remote connection. There is also a portable version, installable on a flash drive, that you can use on public access computers, such as library computers, to connect to your home computers.

CyberGhost. CyberGhost (http://www.cyberghostvpn.com/) is a secure, anonymizing proxy service that uses a "freemium" model (figure 7.7). (This means that the base software is free, but you need to pay in order to access additional services. For example, one of the features you get when you pay is the ability to choose the location of the server you're connecting to.) Once installed and run, all Internet traffic from the user's computer is secured and rerouted through one of CyberGhost's servers around the world. This not only secures the connection but also makes it look like the user's traffic is originating from somewhere other than their actual physical location. While this will slow your traffic down somewhat, it will give you the ability to connect to services more privately and in some cases, you can even connect to services that are not technically available to you based on where you live.

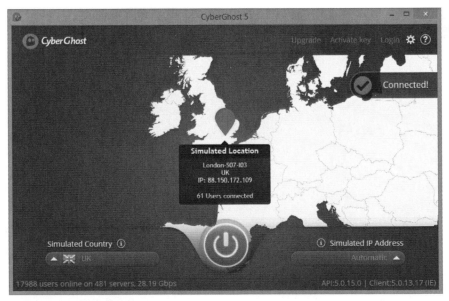

Figure 7.7. CyberGhost.

LIBRARY APPLICATIONS

Now let's take a look at some of the ways in which these technologies might be used in a library beyond what we've already mentioned in our examples.

- Set Chrome to automatically run in Incognito mode on your public access computers by adding *–incognito* to the end of a shortcut. Each browser has a different way to enable privacy automatically; you can search online for instructions for your preferred browser.
- Install the Tor browser as the default browser on public computers or offer it as an option.
- Use Deep Freeze on all of your public computers to ensure patron privacy to your best ability.
- Use LastPass or 1Password yourself and encourage good password practice by your patrons. If you're able, offer the public a class on one of these programs. Jennifer includes password creation as part of her "Be Smart, Not Scared Online" and "Know Your Settings" public computer workshops.
- Encourage integrated library systems (ILS) vendors to allow longer passwords, not just four-digit PINs. Better yet, encourage them to offer a two-factor authentication option for logging in to patron accounts.
- If you're someone who often uses a laptop to connect to open Wi-Fi signals, install and use CyberGhost for some protection, or better yet, install TeamViewer on your laptop and home computer to securely surf the web through your home computer instead of the open Wi-Fi signal.

PRIVACY AND SECURITY EXAMPLES, BY ROBIN HASTINGS, DIRECTOR OF TECHNOLOGY SERVICES, NORTHEAST KANSAS LIBRARY SYSTEM

At the NEKLS (Northeast Kansas Library System) office we have been using Meldium (http://www.meldium.com) as our shared password manager. There are three of us in the IT department who really needed a good, shared manager, and after some trial and error, our network administrator, Ryan Sipes, led us to the free version of Meldium. We needed something that would be online, be easy to use, and would have a browser plug-in that we could use to log in to sites. Meldium hit all those as well as offering private password vaults and apps for both iOS and Android platforms. Meldium works by putting links to what it calls "apps" on a launch pad that is accessible through a website or through a browser plug-in. Once you click on the app, you are automatically taken to the site and logged in. An example would be our NEKLS Amazon account—click on that link and you are taken to Amazon, logged in using our shared purchasing account, and ready to go. I also have an app in my personal vault for Amazon that goes to my personal Amazon account. I can choose to share the link with my coworkers (without giving them access to the password), or I can keep it completely private. Meldium comes with a bunch of applications that you can use—just pick the service, enter your credentials, and we are set. We can also add "custom apps" that go to any website we want, though—for that we just add the URL, enter our credentials, and save!

NOTES

1. "The Heartbleed Bug," Heartbleed, accessed February 27, 2015, http://heart bleed.com/.

2. "Shellshock (software bug)," *Wikipedia*, accessed November 8, 2014, http://en.wikipedia.org/w/index.php?title=Shellshock_(software_bug)&oldid=632634937.

3. "Drupal Community under Attack Due to a Critical SQL Injection Flaw," *Security Affairs* (blog), http://securityaffairs.co/wordpress/29736/cyber-crime/drupal -critical-sql-injection.html.

4. Microsoft, "InPrivate Browsing," Internet Explorer 9, accessed February 27, 2015, http://windows.microsoft.com/en-us/internet-explorer/products/ie-9/features/ in-private.

5. Mozilla Support, "Private Browsing," Firefox, accessed February 27, 2015, https://support.mozilla.org/en-US/kb/private-browsing-browse-web-without-saving -info.

6. Google, "Browse in Private (Incognito Mode)," Chrome Help: Tabs and Windows, accessed February 27, 2015, https://support.google.com/chrome/answer/95464.

7. Apple, "Safari 5.1 (OS X Lion): Browse Privately," Support, accessed February 27, 2015, http://support.apple.com/kb/PH5000.

8. Google, "Browse in Private (Incognito Mode)."

9. Tor, "Tor Project: Anonymity Online," Tor Project, accessed February 27, 2015, https://www.torproject.org/.

10. We would like to stress that installing such software does not remove the need to install antivirus software on those computers. Granted these programs do make it easy to clean up postinfection, but viruses can do damage and/or propagate prior to cleanup, and you should avoid that in the first place.

Chapter Eight

Keeping Up with Emerging Technologies

Up until now, we've been looking at technologies that have existed for years, or at least for the past few months. These tools are "emerging" because they're being used in new ways or are maturing enough to become widely available and mainstream. How do we stay on top of emerging technologies when they are genuinely new, before they move from emerging to maturing? How do we keep a light finger on the pulse of innovation to see what possibilities libraries will have with what's coming next?

The fundamental thing to understand is that you don't need to know everything. The goal is to know about the things that interest, motivate, and compel you and to be aware of as much of the rest as you can.

There are three primary ways to stay on top of emerging technologies, which combine to shape your own professional development:

- Read
- Play
- Teach

READ

The most important thing you can do is read, both print and online, within your field and in the strangest and most unusual places.

Reading to stay on top of emerging technologies doesn't have to be overwhelming. When we say "read," we really mean "skim." You can't read it all in depth, but skimming headlines can be useful all on its own to discover new terms and product names.

Here are some rules of thumb to keep the piles manageable:

- Read as often as you can, and try to set aside time to read every day.
- Use your current "professional reading" schedule and just change the sources for what you read. If you interact with the public, offer trainings, answer reference questions, work with youth of any age, or staff your library's information desk, staying on top of the technologies that your patrons come in asking about is part of your work. Spend work time on work things, including reading.
- Try to read a source relative to its posting frequency: more frequent posts mean that you should be reading that source more frequently.
- Follow links in online sources to additional readings, but be careful of falling down rabbit holes of information. Fifteen minutes can quickly become two hours, and while you may have learned a lot, you've done it at the cost of other work. Balance is key.

Library Sources

The first place you can look for news on emerging technologies is from standard library sources, but probably not ones you're used to looking at. The publications of major library associations and trade journals like *Library Journal* and *School Library Journal* have a library focus, but they aren't necessarily at the cutting edge of our field. Look to these publications for deeper analysis or a view on a maturing technology as it's experimented with and used by libraries.

One field that is closer to the cutting edge is the cross-functional world of the digital humanities: academics, technologists, librarians, archivists, and related professionals exploring the intersection of computing and the humanities. This exploration frequently examines up-and-coming technologies that will have an impact on research, teaching, creation, and preservation (figure 8.1). You can read proceedings and reports from the Association for Computers and the Humanities (www.ach.org) and other members of the Alliance of Digital Humanities Organizations (http://adho.org/) and articles from the *Journal of Digital Humanities* (http://journalofdigitalhumanities.org/) and *Digital Humanities Quarterly* (http://www.digitalhumanities.org/dhq/).

Moving outward, reviewing the schedules and any published proceedings of professional conferences—both in and out of your field of librarianship—can be an excellent source for discovering and seeing the library uses of emerging technologies. There are hundreds of library conferences each year at the local, state, regional, national, and international level in dozens of specialties. You can't possibly attend them all, but you can look at the schedules

Figure 8.1. Articles in the digital humanities often cover useful topics for libraries, from research innovations to ways to use technology in outreach.

of talks and events and see what topics were interesting enough to present. Some conferences will also make handouts, slides, and other presentation materials available even to nonattendees. Over time, you'll develop a short list of conferences to look through and possibly attend; here are a few to get you thinking:

- Library Information and Technology Association (LITA) annual forum (http://www.ala.org/lita/conferences)
- Annual meetings or conferences for state/regional information technology sections (e.g., the information technology section of the New England Library Association, http://nelib.org/connect/sections/its/)
- Code4Lib, a conference for library developers (http://code4lib.org/)
- The Digital Shift, an online event from *Library Journal/School Library Journal* (http://www.thedigitalshift.com/tds)
- Computers in Libraries (http://www.infotoday.com/cil2015/), Internet Librarian (http://internet-librarian.infotoday.com/), and Internet Librarian International (http://www.internet-librarian.com) from Information Today

If there aren't any materials available online at the conference site for a presentation you're interested in, search online for any articles or blog posts written by the speaker—or better still, whitepapers or research findings—about the topic. Search for a company or piece of technology that's mentioned in a talk and learn more about it, then brainstorm to see if it's something that could be used in your own library programming.

Social Media

Crowdsourcing your ability to stay on top of emerging technology is a fantastic use of that same technology. Your friends and family are probably talking about the hot new gadget or app they've discovered; ask them what they like about it, why it's useful and/or fun, and how they found out about it. Explore it yourself, then talk with those friends and family members and see if they can help you come up with library-related ways of using the new gadget or app. Go back to where they first learned about it and follow that source of information for a while just to see how hot it is.

Professional social media connections are an obvious next step. If you don't already have one, create a professional account on Twitter, Facebook, Tumblr, or another platform just to follow interesting library folks, even if you don't post at all (figure 8.2). Don't follow everyone; just start with a few

Figure 8.2.   Following other librarians on social media gives you the benefit of their connections and insights, and it's usually a lot of fun.

library luminaries and see who they mention frequently, then follow those people. Ask your colleagues where they get their tech news and keep tracking back from those sources. Here are a few excellent folks to start with:

- Sarah Houghton (Librarian in Black), http://librarianinblack.net/librarian-inblack/contact/
- Jill Hurst-Wall, http://my.ischool.syr.edu/People/jahurst
- Jason Griffey, http://jasongriffey.net/
- Willie Miller, http://twitter.com/librarywillie
- David Lee King, http://www.davidleeking.com/
- Michael Sauers, http://travelinlibrarian.info/

Geek Sources

Possibly the best—but potentially the most confusing—way to find technology news is to get it from the same places as the computer and Internet professionals do (figure 8.3). The risk is that you'll quickly be overwhelmed by jargon, but the advantage is that these are the resources read by the people inventing the technology you're trying to learn more about. If you know what they know, you're several steps ahead of the game.

Here are some places to get started, but keep in mind that this is only a very small sample of what's out there. Again, follow links to find more obscure, specific, and possibly useful resources.

- Geek/technology news sources such as Gizmodo, Engadget, CNet, Slashdot, ZDNet, TechCrunch, ArsTechnica, and Hacker News (on yCombinator .com)
- Release events from Apple, Microsoft, Google, Amazon, and other large companies are often streamed live on the web for free. Watch these or follow the Twitter chatter to see what's being released in the next few months.
- Trend-watching sites like MacRumors keep tabs on when new products are expected from the major manufacturers and also release sneak peeks of features and designs.
- Academic publications from the large research- or technology-focused universities in the United States and beyond, such as the *MIT Technology Review* (http://www.technologyreview.com/lists/technologies/2014/).

Just like library conferences, technology industry conference schedules and proceedings are a great source of new trends and topics. Again, read through the list of presentations and speakers, look for interesting titles or names that you know, and then search online for the latest news about them.

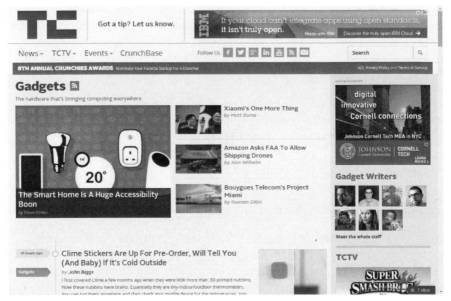

Figure 8.3. Technology news sources like TechCrunch will show you what's cutting edge, as well as an analysis of current trends and new developments in older tech.

- Technology industry conferences: Consumer Electronics Show (CES), Interop (general IT), Macworld, Velocity (web optimization), Defcon (security), NANOG (networks), LISA (system administrators)
- Manufacturer and platform conferences: Apple Worldwide Developers Conference (WWDC), Microsoft's TechEd for developers and IT professionals, Google I/O
- Gaming conventions: E3, Gaming Developers Convention (GDC)
- South by Southwest (SXSW) is a new media/cutting-edge interactive technology conference in Austin, Texas (figure 8.4). It focuses on the intersection of technology, film, music, and culture. Recently, librarians have started attending and speaking at SXSW Interactive; in 2012, Nate Hill, Amy Buckland, Char Booth, and Michael Porter spoke on libraries and community publishing (http://schedule.sxsw.com/2012/events/event_IAP9273).

You can also search online for lists of recommended conferences for entrepreneurs and geeks of all stripes, such as The Next Web's list of must-attend conferences for 2014 (http://thenextweb.com/entrepreneur/2014/01/04/10-must-attend-tech-conferences-2014/).

Figure 8.4. SXSW brings together new media/interactive technology innovations from all parts of the field, offering a wide variety of inspirations and potential services and tools.

Popular and Mainstream Sources

Many mainstream and popular media outlets are now full of news about emerging technologies, the latest apps, and most important, how average people use these products and tools. Whatever your current popular reading consists of, it can probably help you stay aware of what's coming from a much more practical point of view. A few sources are more consistently reporting on technology news and new gadgets:

- *New York Times*, *Washington Post*, *SF Chronicle*, and other major newspapers
- CNN or the British Broadcasting Company (BBC) on television and online
- *Time*, *Atlantic*, *Newsweek*, and other news magazines, including spin-off publications and sites like the *Atlantic*'s CityLab (http://www.citylab.com/)
- The *Economist*, especially its "Technology Quarterly" and some of the special reports
- Online news sources such as the *Huffington Post*

Even popular magazines like *Women's Day*, *Car & Driver*, and *Cook's Illustrated* include technology/gadget/app sections. If you subscribe to them yourself, or if your library gets them, you can skim them for ideas, especially since these publications are probably where your patrons are learning about the technology.

Less-Obvious Sources

These last few ideas for information about emerging technologies might seem a little far-fetched, but the most interesting things often come from more obscure origins.

In the crowdfunding chapter, we looked at how libraries are using platforms like Kickstarter and Indiegogo to raise money for programs, services, and technology. Many new and revolutionary technologies are being funded in the same way. By skimming new campaigns and projects on these sites, you might find the early prototypes of a product that changes the world two years from now.

If you haven't yet watched a TED or TEDx talk, we strongly recommend that you do. "Ideas worth spreading" is the program's tagline, and while many of those ideas are philosophical or involve higher math, many of the talks give a voice to real people solving real problems or coming up with real solutions in incredibly innovative ways. Filter the search to technology and you'll see the amazing diversity of what's available to listen to and watch.

Most unexpected of all might be your own hobbies, creative pursuits, and other interests. Remember, the personal computer began as an electronics hobby—Steve Jobs and Steve Wozniak were computer hobbyists who started Apple Computers in Jobs's garage. What do you see happening in the hobbies that you're passionate about? The next disruptive technology could be being born under your nose.

PLAY

As library technology trainers, we frequently tell our participants that the only way to truly learn a new tool (or technology) is to use it and, in particular, to play with it. Playing with technology removes the need to feel like you've mastered it, and it opens you up to seeing the possibilities of how it can be useful to you, your library, and your patrons.

Whenever possible, get your hands on a new piece of technology and see how it works (figure 8.5). Most technology retail stores from the Apple Store to Best Buy to the newer Microsoft Stores all encourage you to pick up devices and play with them in order to see which one suits you best. Use these stores as field research to see what's going to be in the hands of the people who walk through your library's doors.

Figure 8.5. To truly learn a gadget or an online tool, you have to get your hands on it and play.

If you have friends who either work in the tech industry or are always buying the hot new thing, invite them over for dinner and ask them to bring their favorite new gadget for you to play with. They'll be happy to talk about it and tell you just why it's going to change everything. For instance, Jennifer found out about Google Cardboard (see chapter 3) when a friend brought his to a summer barbecue and let everyone try it out. Here are a few suggestions for learning about a new tool or device:

- *Read about it online.* Before you pick it up, see what others think of it and what you should be on the lookout for.
- *Read the screen.* Many devices come with only the most basic of print instructions now, and everything you need to know about it is available somewhere on the device itself.
- *Push the buttons.* Just looking at a device will tell you very little about how it can be used or what its potential is. Start pushing buttons, especially on display models, and see what you can do.
- *Take your time.* This is professional development, just like your reading and training are. Give it the time it deserves and really put the gadget through its paces.
- *Don't be afraid.* Be respectful of other people's property, but realize that you can't learn a new tool if you're afraid to use it.

- *Do the "driving" yourself.* You get a much better sense of how something works when you use it with your own hands. Don't just watch someone else—get in there and use it yourself.
- *Write about it.* Whether you blog online, write an internal e-mail, or simply jot down your own thoughts, express what you've discovered about the technology to someone else and put your ideas into words. If you can talk or write about what you've experienced, you're more likely to understand what it is you've learned.

One way to do all of these things is to participate in—or run—a professional development program based on the "23 Things" model developed by the Public Library of Charlotte and Mecklenburg in 2006. This online, blog-based learning program encouraged participants to try new "web 2.0" tools and write about the experience. If your library or regional system isn't running this kind of program, check out Nebraska Learns 2.0: an ongoing program co-coordinated by Michael (http://nlcblogs.nebraska.gov/nelearns/). Or create a list of gadgets and platforms you'd like to try out, work through them a week at a time, and post your experiences online.

TEACH

One further step to learning and staying on top of new technologies is teaching others about them. After you've read and played and you feel you understand a new piece of technology, offer to run a workshop about it for your library's staff or the public. Use what you've learned and get a deeper understanding of the technology by trying to explain it to others. Before you decide to teach a class on a new bit of technology, ask yourself:

- What do you know you know?
- What do you think you know?
- What do you know you don't know?

For what you know you know and what you think you know, research a little and read a few articles or books. Are you right? Do you have the facts and the basics straight? If you know one way to use a piece of technology, do other people have very different ideas? Can you include (and credit) their ideas and your own? What surprises do you find?

While you're researching, keep another list of what you have discovered that you didn't already know. If your original list of what you don't know plus these new additions is bigger than the list of what you do know, don't do the class until you've learned and practiced some more. Trying to teach a class when you're not entirely sure of the materials is frustrating for you and for your students.

If you decide you're going to learn about something in order to teach it, make sure you can deliver on that promise. Give yourself plenty of time to build on the basics and learn much more about the topic than you'd ever present in class. Your students will surprise you with the questions they ask, and while you can't possibly predict all of them, the more you've prepared the better off you'll be.

Here is a checklist to go through before you teach a class, with some examples from Jennifer's perpetual Facebook class for the public.

- You need to know more about a technology or tool to teach it than just to use it. While Jennifer might not use Facebook groups or paid ads herself, she needs to know something about them in case that's what someone in the class is interested in.
- Can you respond to the random questions? For example, "How can I keep someone from posting obscene things?"
- Can you give additional details to the advanced students? For example, beginning students may be happy just posting status updates and sharing other posts, but more advanced folks want to download images, set up pages, and create groups.
- Can you suggest next steps after your workshop? There are too many Facebook settings to review in one workshop, so Jennifer highlights the most important ones for beginners and suggests sitting down with a cup of tea (or something stronger) and going through them all section by section.
- Do you have a goal for your students? For example, should they end the class having signed up for Facebook, know enough about it to decide whether they *want* to sign up, or be able to more smoothly use the Facebook account they already have?

Finally, in class, listen closely to the questions that your participants ask and the ideas that they come up with. A random comment by an older woman learning about Facebook might lead you to a new marketing campaign. Inspiration can come from anywhere.

PROFESSIONAL DEVELOPMENT

Every technique we've discussed so far and every resource we've looked at in this book will help you continue your professional development around emerging technologies. However, more traditional professional development opportunities certainly improve the mix.

Most libraries, library systems, and library associations offer classes, workshops, and conference tracks on technology and more of them are including topics like "What's Next?" "The Next Big Thing," or "Coming Trends in Library Technology." If your organization isn't offering these classes, ask for them! There's always part of a postevent survey that asks about future topics—write down a list of the gadgets and ideas you find in your reading and write them in on the next survey you fill out.

Switching to online resources, Lynda.com (http://www.lynda.com/) has been offering self-paced video-based tutorials on business, software, and design skills and technologies for the past twenty years. You can sign up for an individual membership ($25/month or less at the time of writing) or ask your library to subscribe with a group membership for all staff. A newer player in the library online training field is Gale Courses (http://solutions.cengage .com/GaleCourses/) from Gale/Cengage. Gale Courses has a wider variety of topics than Lynda.com, and uses a synchronous time–based class structure that might better suit your learning style. If your library offers Lynda.com or Gale Courses to the public, take advantage of your own library services for your professional development.

If your community has centers for adult education or continuing education programs at local colleges or universities, you might find that they offer courses that will keep you thinking of the future. Platforms like edX (http:// www.edx.org/) and Coursera (http://www.coursera.org/) provide free access to the online versions of courses from international-level schools like Harvard, MIT, CalTech, the École Polytechnique, Kyoto University, and more. By using these resources, you're learning the same things as many patrons who will be coming to you with questions, and in addition to your own learning, you'll be better poised to answer those questions.

Finally, look beyond library- or academic-oriented training. Retailers like the Apple (http://www.apple.com/retail/learn/) and Microsoft (http://www .microsoft.com/en-us/store/locations/personal-training) stores, Verizon Wireless (http://www.verizonwireless.com/workshop/) and other mobile device stores, and others offer classes (often free) on the devices and software they sell. At Best Buy, the Geek Squad will provide on-site training and help for a fee (http://www.geeksquad.com/services/computers/training.aspx), and they have a great library of do-it-yourself tips and tricks on their website (http:// www.geeksquad.com/do-it-yourself/).

CONCLUSION

Our goal for this book was to demonstrate how to look at any new or evolving piece of technology and evaluate it in terms of library service and the needs of library users. We also hoped to give you ideas for ways to stay on top of the avalanche of innovation occurring daily throughout the world. Even in the course of writing this, we needed to revise sections as gadgets were discontinued and as startlingly disruptive tools were released.

There will always be something new to learn about, some advance that changes everything. The hope is that continuous awareness and evaluation helps libraries find a place on the crest of the wave, surfing high with a grand view of what's next.

Index

About the Authors

Jennifer Koerber is the public instruction curriculum development coordinator for the Boston Public Library and an independent trainer and speaker on emerging technologies and the social web. She is a self-hacked tech librarian and has observed how people interact with technology for more than fifteen years as a children's librarian, reference librarian, library branch manager, web services librarian, and now trainer. She earned her MSLIS from Simmons College in 1998. She has written several articles on library innovation and self-publishing for libraries for *Library Journal* and *The Digital Shift* and has been training the public in technology and online life for twelve years. Visit www.jenniferkoerber.com for a full list of her presentations and publications.

Michael P. Sauers is the director of technology for Do Space (DoSpace.org) in Omaha, Nebraska, and has been training librarians in technology for the past twenty years. He has been a public library trustee, bookstore manager for a library friends group, reference librarian, serials cataloger, technology consultant, and bookseller. He earned his MLS in 1995 from the University at Albany's School of Information Science and Policy. Michael's thirteenth book, *Google Search Secrets*, was published in October 2013, and more books are on the way. He has also written dozens of articles for various journals and magazines. In his spare time, he blogs at travelinlibrarian.info, runs websites for authors and historical societies, takes many photos, and reads more than one hundred books a year.